JACOB'S LADDER

PETER KREEFT

JACOB'S LADDER

Ten Steps to Truth

IGNATIUS PRESS   SAN FRANCISCO

Cover painting by Stephen Dudro

Cover design by Riz Boncan Marsella

© 2013 by Ignatius Press, San Francisco
All rights reserved
ISBN 978-1-58617-732-4
Library of Congress Control Number 2012942804
Printed in the United States of America ∞

CONTENTS

INTRODUCTION

As a Catholic and an author of some seventy books, I am often asked by journalists for "the Catholic perspective" on this or that. But there is no such thing as "the Catholic perspective"—not because Catholicism is too soft and flexible to have a single perspective but because it is too hard and dogmatic to be a "perspective". There is "the masculine perspective" and "the feminine perspective", "the conservative perspective" and "the liberal perspective", but there is no such thing as "the Catholic perspective". Catholicism is not a "perspective". It is the truth, the facts, the divinely Authorized *data*.

Why any honest, logical, and intelligent person in the twenty-first century would believe such an unfashionable dogma—why they could believe there was any such thing as "dogma"—that is the question the journalist should be asking, for that is the question behind the question, the story behind the story. This book is about that question.

It is really ten questions. The ten are in a logical order, and the answer to each one is a matter of logic, of reason, not faith. This book is addressed to an intelligent, open-minded Martian. Would that *New York Times* journalists were open-minded Martians!

Because questions are best answered by dialogue, by comparing two sides of the question, I have written ten dialogues about the ten most basic questions you can ask.

Because a dialogue is not just two "points of view" or two philosophies but a conversation between two different people, I give you here not only two philosophies but two persons. They are both fictional. They are taken from my fictional non-novel *An Ocean Full of Angels* (Saint Augustine's Press, 2010). The last time I used two of the characters from this fiction, in *A Refutation of Moral Relativism*, half the readers thought they were real, not fictional. I apologize for the confusion, and I thank you for the compliment.

PASSION

It was 1977. Libby Rawls had just resigned from the Department of Social Services, and for the first time in her adult life she had nothing to do but enjoy the beach for the rest of the summer. She smiled at the little waves that were lapping happily at the wet, chocolate-colored sand and making music with the tiny stones by rattling them together. She smiled at the sun sparkling on the water's wrinkles. It was a perfect August day at Nahant Beach, just north of Boston.

Libby was only twenty-three, but she had already entered and exited freelance journalism and detective work, as well as social services. She was now "burnt out" and cynical, after repeatedly butting heads with bureaucracy at the Massachusetts Department of Social Services.

Strange people had often fallen into her unpredictable life, and "Mother" was only the latest one. Libby never discovered how or why she received that name, but no one ever thought to call her anything else. Libby thought of her as a "universal woman", not only because of her mixed race (she was part Jewish, part Hawaiian-Polynesian, and part African) but because her size and shape reminded her of the whole planet. Like a limousine, she occupied two ordinary parking spaces. Her six-foot chassis weighed well over three hundred pounds, but it was all muscle and no flab. This was modestly covered by a bathing suit, which itself was covered by immodestly bright yellow, green, red, and blue figures of toucans.

As Libby arrived at the beach, she was drawn, like a moon, to this planetary body, which was sitting in an oversized beach chair on a bright red blanket. Though the beach was over a mile long, it was crowded today, and much of the crowd was cheering an impromptu waterside performance by two black men, "Diddly" and "Squat", who were putting on the most hilarious and unclassifiable athletic dance performance she had ever seen. Diddly was almost seven feet tall, thin and rubbery, and Squat was half that height but as wide as he was tall; so Diddly was dribbling Squat like a basketball, to the boom-box strains of Spike Jones' "Mister Lee", and the whole beach, including Mother, was cheering and laughing.

Watching Diddly and Squat, Libby felt a delight that she had missed for many months, and her delight and amazement was squared when the two of them bounced up to Mother's blanket after their performance. Libby discovered that they both lived with Mother at a rooming house on Nahant, and that Diddly was deaf and Squat blind. "He's my eyes, and I'm his ears", Squat said.

Libby resolved to get to know these two unpredictable creatures better, but today they were rushing off for a gig that evening. The scraps of information Mother told Libby about herself, about Diddly and Squat, and about the other boarders in her house on Nahant tasted like appetizers to Libby, and she immediately accepted Mother's invitation to visit "The House" soon.

Libby noticed that Mother was reading a book with the words "Catholic" and "sex" in the title. "What's that book about?" Libby asked.

"Do you really want to know, or are you just making polite conversation?" Mother asked, bluntly. As Libby increasingly discovered, Mother was refreshingly (or was it uncomfortably?) blunt.

"Since you asked the honest question, I'll give you the honest answer", Libby replied. "I really don't know."

Mother looked up with a smile of surprise. "Honesty. That's my best friend, I think. I like you, girl. I suspect you know some things about the rules of thinking."

"What do you mean, 'the rules of thinking'?"

"I think you know you can't just plunge into something like that, any more than you can just plunge into the sea whenever you want. You have to do all sorts of things first."

"What things?"

"Well, you have to get there first. You know. Plan the trip. Get the money. Wait for summer. Change your clothes. Get in the car. Gas it up. Drive to the beach. Park the car. Put on the sunscreen. Go where the water is. Only then can you plunge in."

"You mean it takes that kind of preparation to understand that book?"

"Yup."

"Must be an unusual book."

"Nope. A lot of good books are that way. Like a ladder. You get the view only from the top, but to get to the top you have to climb up the rungs, one at a time."

"So what's the first rung?"

"You really want to know?"

"Sure."

"Now?"

"Why not?"

"So you're not just making polite conversation?"

"No."

"Well, good for you, girl. You put your foot on the first rung right there."

"What do you mean? What 'first rung'?"

"Do you have a passion to know? That's the first rung."

"A *passion*? It has to be a passion? It can't just be an *interest*?"

"No. An 'interest'—what's that, anyway? Sounds to me like a euphemism for 'just making polite conversation'."

"But 'a passion'—that sounds a little . . . well, fanatical."

"Oooh! You said the F-word!"

Libby laughed. "'Fundamentalist' is my F-word."

"And that means pretty much the same thing to you, right?"

"Right. But not to you?"

"Oh, I'm not into the Fs. I'm into the Ps. Passion. That's what I'm talking about."

"Passion. That sounds sexy."

"It is, in a way. But I'm talking about the passion for truth."

"Okay, even though it doesn't sound as thrilling as sex."

"Oh, but sometimes it is. That can be a kind of quasi-sexual thrill too, you know, when truth enters your mind's body."

"'Your mind's body'? Isn't that a confusion of categories?"

"Not if we listen to our language. We use the same word for it when it happens to the mind as when it happens to the body."

"'Orgasm', you mean?"

"I was thinking of the word for the thing that results *from* it."

"What word?"

"Conception."

"Huh. Never thought of that. So you're saying that the mind is like the body, and the body has its passions, so the mind does too? And the mind makes mind-babies just as the body makes body-babies? Yeah, I guess that's logical."

"It *is* logical. But is it personal?"

"What do you mean?"

"Is *your* passion?"

"Is *what* my passion?"

"Truth."

"No, I think not. Why should I have a 'passion' for two plus two make four, or for how many shells are on this beach?"

"What about bigger truths?"

"You mean like the stuff in that book? God and religion and all?"

"Right."

"I'm not an atheist, but I'm kinda skeptical of organized religion."

"I'm not talking about 'organized religion'—whatever that is."

"What do you mean, 'whatever that is'? Where are you from, woman? Mars? What do you mean?"

"I mean that all the religion I've ever seen on this planet looks more like *dis*organized religion. But what I mean about a passion for truth—I don't mean only about religion, but I don't mean two plus two make four either. I mean death and life." Mother reached into her beach bag and came up with another book. "*This* is what I mean by a passion for truth. Just do me a favor and read this one page. Just indulge me for a minute, okay? Because I think this is you."

Libby looked at the title of the book. It was Pascal's *Pensées*.

"Why? Where is this book going to take me? What is its agenda? And why should I care?"

"No, it's not *its* agenda, it's *your* agenda you should care about. '*Pensées*' means 'thoughts'. It's about a journey of thought, and I think you are already on such a journey. I think you have already made the first step, and this passage is about that first step, which is a passion to know. So I think you will recognize yourself in it."

Libby was skeptical but intrigued. So she took up the book. Mother explained, "He's talking about the mystery of death, and how nobody knows what will happen to him when he dies, but we should at least *care* even if we don't *know*." Libby read the marked passage, where Pascal says that the question of death

is something of such vital importance to us, affecting us so deeply, that one must have lost all feeling not to care about knowing the facts of the matter. All our actions and thoughts must follow such different paths according to whether there is hope of eternal blessings or not, that the only possible way of acting with sense and judgment is to decide our course in the light of this point, which ought to be our ultimate objective.

And that is why, amongst those who are not convinced, I make an absolute distinction between those who strive with all their might to learn and those who live without troubling themselves or thinking about it.

I can feel nothing but compassion for those who sincerely lament their doubt, who regard it as the ultimate misfortune, and who, sparing no effort to escape from it, make their search their principal and most serious business.

But as for those who spend their lives without a thought for this final end of life and who, solely because they do not find within themselves the light of conviction, neglect to look elsewhere, and to examine thoroughly whether this opinion is one of those which people accept out of credulous simplicity or one of those which, though obscure in themselves, nonetheless have a most solid and unshakable foundation: as for them, I view them very differently.

This negligence in a matter where they themselves, their eternity, their all are at stake, fills me more with irritation than pity; it astounds and appalls me; it seems quite monstrous to me. I do not say this prompted by the pious zeal of spiritual devotion. I mean on the contrary that we ought to have this feeling from principles of human interest and self-esteem. For that we need only see what the least enlightened see.

One needs no great sublimity of soul to realize that in this life there is no true and solid satisfaction, that all our pleasures are mere vanity, that our afflictions are infinite, and finally that death which threatens us at every moment must in a few years infallibly face us with the inescapable and appalling alternative of being annihilated or wretched throughout eternity.

Nothing could be more real or more dreadful than that. Let us put on as bold a face as we like: that is the end awaiting the world's most illustrious life . . .

It is therefore quite certainly a great evil to have such doubts, but it is at least an indispensable obligation to seek when one does thus doubt; so the doubter who does not seek is at the same time very unhappy and very wrong. If in addition he feels a calm satisfaction, which he openly professes, and even regards as a reason for joy and vanity, I can find no terms to describe so extravagant a creature.

What can give rise to such feelings? What reason for joy can be found in the expectation of nothing but helpless wretchedness? What reason for vanity in being plunged into impenetrable darkness? And how can such an argument as this occur to a reasonable man?

"I do not know who put me into the world, nor what the world is, not what I am myself.... I see the terrifying spaces of the universe hemming me in, and I find myself attached to one corner of this vast expanse without knowing why I have been put in this place rather than that, or why the brief span of life allotted to me should be assigned to one moment rather than another of all the eternity which went before me and all that which will come after me. I see only infinity on every side, hemming me in like an atom or like the shadow of a fleeting instant. All I know is that I must soon die, but what I know least about is this very death which I cannot evade.

"Just as I do not know whence I come, so I do not know whither I am going. All I know is that when I leave this world I shall fall for ever into nothingness, or into the hands of a wrathful God, but I do not know which of these two states is to be my eternal lot. Such is my state, full of weakness and uncertainty. And my conclusion from all this is that I must pass my days without a thought of seeking what is to happen to me. Perhaps I might find some enlightenment in my doubts, but I do not want to take the trouble, nor take a step to look for it; and afterwards, as I sneer at those who are striving to this end.... I will go without fear or foresight to face so momentous an event, and allow myself to be carried off limply to my death, uncertain of my future state for all eternity."

Who would wish to have as his friend a man who argued like that? Who would choose him from among others as a confidant in his affairs? Who would resort to him in adversity? To what use in life could he possibly be turned?

It is truly glorious for religion to have such unreasonable men as enemies.*

---

* Blaise Pascal, *Pensées*, trans. A.J. Krailsheimer (London: Penguin Classics, 1995), p. 427.

Libby finished and put the book down. Mother wondered: What was that look on her face? Puzzled? Wistful? Annoyed? Embarrassed? Rueful? Just thoughtful?

"Well?"

"It's powerful", Libby admitted. "But it didn't convert me."

"That's not what he's trying to do. He's just trying to *worry* you."

"Hey, I didn't come to the beach to be worried!"

"*You* don't think you did. But are you sure Fate didn't bring you here for that?"

"To be worried?"

"Yeah, to be worried. Do you think this just *happened*? Of all the beaches in the world, how many of them contain a lady with a copy of Pascal in her beach bag?"

"You're very direct."

"Like Pascal, I hope."

"And you say he's not trying to convert me. Are you?"

"Nope. Only trying to worry you. To get you to put that first foot on the ladder. To be *sensible*."

"You mean to be religious."

"No, I mean to be sensible. And therefore to be passionate. Because 'Nothing great has ever been accomplished without passion.' "

"I know that quote! It's from Hegel's *Philosophy of History*."

"Wow. Not one person in a thousand knows that. You must believe it, if you remembered it. Especially from Hegel, of all people."

"But I'm not a Hegel fan. I never even read him, just that quote."

"You're lucky."

"He was a cosmic optimist. I'm not. I've been knocked around too often by life to trust it much."

"So get mad at life, if you have to. Hate life if you can't love it. But care. Have passion. Hate is closer to love than indifference is, you know. You can love and hate the same person at the same time; and I think you can do that to life too."

"I know that. I was a psychology major. But I'm not in love with religion."

"Fine, hate religion too, if you can't love it. Just don't patronize it; don't treat it as a nice story about a giant Santa Claus that keeps grown-up children quiet and good."

"Frankly, I suspect that *is* what it is most of the time. I wonder whether religion isn't just the world's biggest fairy tale."

"Fine, be an agnostic, then, if you will, or even an atheist, but be an honest and passionate one. If you honestly think religion is just a fairy tale, then expose it. But don't patronize it, or the people who believe it. Wake them up if you think it's a dream."

"Maybe we only wake up from one dream to another. How do I know life isn't just one big dream?"

"Because you can do things. You can make a difference. You can choose. You can't do anything in a dream except dream."

"Sometimes we'd rather dream than wake up. Sometimes reality hurts; truth hurts, waking hurts."

"How?"

"Sometimes it exposes you. It shows up your dark side. That's why Nietzsche hated it. You know, he once wrote, 'Why truth? Why not rather untruth?'"

"But Nietzshe had passion, at least, even though it was a dark passion. He rose to the dignity of despair."

"But he chose the lie over the truth."

"Yes, but at least he had passion. He was a liar instead of a lawyer."

"He was almost a Nazi."

"But he wasn't a pop psychologist."

"He hated truth."

"But he didn't patronize it."

"He wanted to murder truth. He wanted to murder God. He said we killed God because God was truth, because God saw his dark side. God was his *victim*."

"Yes—and he gave his victim the honor of caring about whether He lived or died. That's more than some polite religious people do."

"Oh. But—isn't truth the very first thing?"

"No. I think *a passion for it* is the very first thing. Because if you don't have that passion, if you don't care about it, if you don't seek it, then you won't find it."

"So even Nietzsche knew the very first thing, the first rung on the ladder."

"Yes."

"Even though he wanted to murder truth."

"Yes. Better be a murderer of truth than a patronizer of it. Better fight against the light, if you won't fight against the darkness, but at least fight. Care. Fight for the wrong side if you can't fight for the right side, but don't stand on the sidelines and sneer at the game. Have blood in your veins, not tepid water."

"You know, you don't sound like most religious people."

"I guess you've never read Pascal. Or Dostoyevski. Or Augustine's *Confessions*."

"No, I haven't. Why do you think I should?"

"Because if you do, you will be moved."

"To what? To religion?"

"Not necessarily. Maybe to envy."

"Envy?"

"Envy of their passion, and shame at your lack of it. That's how most readers are moved, I think."

"Augustine was the playboy of the Western world, wasn't he?"

"He had two great passions: sex and truth, heat and light. He was a passionate man."

"But he gave up sex for God, right?"

"But he never gave up passion. Medieval statues of Augustine always have him holding a book in one hand and a burning heart in the other."

"So you're putting Augustine and Nietzsche together on the side of passion. What an unusual team! Next thing, I guess you'll put Jesus and Hitler together?"

"Sure! How did Hitler win Germany? How did he almost win the world? By his passion. By Step One. But no Step Two for him. No truth. You see, passion alone is a blind power. It's fire without light. It just ignites *whatever* it touches, good or evil, truth or lies, unselfishness or selfishness, love or lust. That's why it's dangerous to stop on Step One. But just imagine what a saint Hitler would have made if he had gone on and put all that passion into love instead of hate."

"What a great plot for a fantasy novel! Just imagine ..."

"And just imagine what would happen if all the passion of lust was redirected to love and all the energy of self-deception to the search for truth. Just imagine what would happen if our whole culture did that. Now there's a great plot for you."

"How can we have a kind of sexual passion for something as abstract as truth?"

"What do you think truth is?"

"Everybody knows what truth is. Truth is telling it like it is. Having your thoughts match the facts, having your sentences match the universe. How can the desire for something that abstract rival the desire for sex? It's ridiculous."

"That is, yes. But truth is more than that. It's not just a correct relationship between abstract thought and concrete reality. I think it's a *personal* relationship—in fact it's a *sexual* relationship between us and reality."

"Sexual?"

"Yes. To know truth is to be impregnated, to become pregnant in your mind. Truth is the mind's lover, the mind's husband."

"I never thought of truth that way. But what is truth to a man then? A homosexual relationship?"

"No, because homosexuals don't get pregnant. It's a heterosexual relationship to men too—all men—because our minds are all female. All minds are wombs."

"So reality is the man and our mind is the woman, and he impregnates us, and we conceive a concept?"

"Yes. And the baby resembles both parents. Our concept of an apple resembles its father the physical apple because it's red and tart and fruity, but it also resembles its mother the mind because it's mental rather than physical."

"I think most people picture truth as coming into their eyes, not into their wombs. We learn through the organs between our ears, not the one between our legs."

"The brain, you mean?"

"And the eyes. The point is that truth is like light, not like sex."

"And you think that makes it less passionate?"

"Of course. Light is pale and cool and abstract compared to sex."

"Tell that to someone blind."

"Oops."

"Or remember when you were young enough to be really, really scared of the dark, and then someone shone a light."

"But we don't usually have a sexual passion for *concepts.*"

"No, and we don't usually have a sexual passion for babies either. We have a sexual passion for the beauty of our partner and for the joy of the experience. But babies come from it all the same. And so do concepts."

"Hmmm . . . I never realized there were so many tunnels between the bedroom and the classroom."

"And what do those tunnels mean? That the fire of a quasi-sexual passion can be directed at truth; that the light of truth can be the object of passion."

"Mother, let me be totally honest with you. You fascinate me, but I'm skeptical of where I think you're taking me. If I get on your ladder now, you're probably going to take me up to Heaven, and I don't want to go there."

"You don't *know* that. You only *fear* that. Are you going to let fear lead you?"

"I told you, I'm skeptical of religion. I don't find it fascinating. You do, maybe. Fine. But I'm not you."

"You were fascinated by Diddly and Squat a few minutes ago. Your passion caught fire. I saw it in your eyes. Am I right?"

"Yeah, so what?"

"If two dancers can do that, don't you think God— the real, live God—might be able to do it even more?"

"Maybe. I don't know. I don't claim to know anything about religion."

"Okay. Start there. Start where you are. You don't know yet whether you should be a skeptic or a rationalist, an atheist or a theist, a Muslim or a Christian, a Protestant or a Catholic. But you do know one thing: you should be a woman, not a jellyfish."

At this point, a wave deposited a small jellyfish on the corner of their blanket. Libby looked up at the sky. "Now that's spooky!" she said, laughing. "But I'll admit this much, Mother: I'll admit that there's one chance in a hundred that that jellyfish was a sign from God. So I think I will take that chance. Can we continue this conversation tomorrow?"

"Sure can, girl. Same time, same beach. Congratulations for getting a little taller. You put a foot on the ladder, you know."

Dialogue Two

TRUTH

Mother arrived early at the beach, but Libby was already there, even though the day was cloudy. "So!" Mother said, as she plunked her blanket down. "You said Yes to Step One. You've got the passion to know. That's why you're here, right? You won't find much sun on the beach today, so I guess you came for the other kind of light, yes?"

"I guess so."

"So let's talk about the second rung."

"I guess I'm in the market, Mother, but I'm skeptical."

"Skeptical of what?"

"Of ever finding the thing I've decided to care about. Truth."

"Ah. Good for you."

"Good to be a skeptic?"

"No, good to see what the next logical question is. First love, then hope. You've decided to love the truth, and now you wonder whether you have any hope of finding it."

"Right."

"So let's take on skepticism today. Let's look at the reasons *for* it. What do you think is the strongest reason to be a skeptic?"

Libby thought for a few seconds, then answered, "Honesty. Humility. Self-knowledge. We humans are just too stupid and too weak to find what we're looking for. That's why we keep looking. And anybody who thinks they *have* found it and *stops* looking for it is an arrogant, dogmatic fool."

"That sounds like a good argument to me. But it has a hidden premise that's false, I think. And that premise is common to both the skeptic and the dogmatist. Do you see it?"

"No. Maybe my premise microscope is out of focus. What do *you* see there?"

"The assumption that truth is a *thing*, a zero-sum thing, an all-or-nothing thing, so that you either simply have it or you don't. Like a rock. Isn't it more like sunlight? Look at today. It's cloudy, so you can't see the sun. Yet you *can* see the sunlight through the clouds, if you're not blind. It's not nighttime, after all. And it's getting brighter and brighter."

"Okay, so we can know cloudy truth. But we want to see sunny truth. We're not satisfied. We're not happy."

"And that's good skepticism, I think. Always distrust a happy skeptic, I say. A happy skeptic is a dogmatic skeptic. She's not a truth-seeker any more. She's given up. Skepticism is her home. But that's not you, I think. You're an unhappy skeptic. Skepticism is not your home; it's your launching pad."

"In other words, an unhappy skeptic is a truth-seeker."

"Exactly."

"So where do I go from here? How do I know skepticism won't turn out to be my home too? How do I refute it?"

"That's easy."

"Easy?"

"Yes, easy. It contradicts itself. It says, 'The truth is that there is no truth', or 'I know that I don't know', or 'I'm certain that there's no certainty.' "

"What about a sort of semi-skepticism, like today's clouds? Let's say the night is like simple skepticism, and the sunlight is like certain knowledge, and the cloudy light is like less-than-certain knowledge, *probable* knowledge. Maybe all our knowledge is only probable. Maybe the sun will never come out in our minds as it will come out in the sky."

"If all knowledge is only probable, do you *know* that? And is *that* knowledge certain?"

"No, it's only probable. Otherwise I contradict myself again."

"But if it's only probable, then maybe it isn't true, maybe the sun *will* come out. So you *can* have hope."

"I see. Whatever kind of skepticism I have, I have to be skeptical of my skepticism."

"Gotcha!"

"What do you mean, 'Gotcha'? You got me? Are we playing tag with each other?"

"No, no, I mean *you* have the right to say, 'Gotcha!' now—like when you shine a light onto someone's face who's been hiding."

"And the face is the face of skepticism."

"Gotcha!"

"Well, maybe not. Let's look more closely."

"Yes, let's."

"Suppose I say we do know the truth, but all truth is relative. There are as many truths as there are people, and needs, and circumstances, and they're all different."

"So truth is a kind of 'whatever'."

"Yeah. It's flexible. Relativism."

"So where skepticism says truth is a wild-goose chase, relativism says it's a jelly."

"You can't refute an idea by calling it names."

"Oh, I know that. I'm not trying to refute it, just trying to pin it down."

"But you can't do that to a jelly."

"My point exactly."

"But jelly is real. It just takes the shape of its container."

"Yes. Truth becomes '*my* truth' or '*your* truth'".

"What's wrong with that?"

"What's wrong with that is that if that's true, then nobody is ever wrong. Simple skepticism says nobody is ever right, and relativism says nobody is ever wrong. And that's just as self-contradictory as saying nobody is ever right. Because if nobody is ever wrong, then the person who says relativism is wrong isn't wrong either!"

"Maybe that's right. Maybe nobody's wrong."

"In other words, 'Don't be judgmental.' "

"Right."

"That's your absolute, then: that relativism. Absolutely no absolutes! And you're being judgmental against being judgmental. So you're still contradicting yourself."

"Oops."

"I'll take that for what Catholics call a 'short act of contrition'."

"Wait. Maybe we each create our own truth, our own world, our own reality. Maybe it's like Edgar Allen Poe said: 'Is all that we see or seem / But a dream within a dream?' "

"So now truth isn't a jelly but a dream."

"Yes. Why not?"

"So all communication is just sharing our dreams with each other."

"Yes. Why not?"

"But not *really* sharing dreams, only dreaming that we do."

"I feel another 'Oops' coming."

"The same one. Logical self-contradiction. If truth is only subjective, then it's not objectively true that truth is only subjective. It's just your dream. And if I claim to be awake and not dreaming, then you have nothing to say to me. Because if you say that my claim is false, that I'm not really awake but only dreaming, then you're claiming to know what's really, objectively true, not just what you're dreaming."

"Oops."

"So are you satisfied we've refuted skepticism?"

"I guess we have—all forms of it."

"Not quite. Suppose Kant is right?"

"Kant?"

"Kant. He called his 'big idea' the 'Copernican revolution in philosophy'. He said that we're not in *individual* dreams but a kind of collective, shared dream. That our common world is created by a kind of common, universal reason. That we project all our categories like a movie projector onto a blank screen, instead of discovering them."

"What categories?"

"All categories. Including time and space and logical relations like causality, and concepts like God and self and world. If Kant is right, we're making that movie all the time. So that is a kind of skepticism—of our ability to know objective reality, what Kant called 'things in themselves'. Do you know why *that* kind of skepticism is self-contradictory too?"

"I think so. If that's true, then what's the blank screen? And how can you know *that*?"

"You see the logic."

"And if the self is only one of those subjective categories in the dream, who's the dreamer? God? Am I nothing but His dream? Or yours? Or my own? No, that won't work. If Kant's right, we can't ever know objective truth. But is it an objective truth that we can't know objective truth? And is it an objective truth that truth is not objective but constructed? If it is, then he contradicts himself. If it's not, then we're in an infinite hall of mirrors: it's only a construction that truth is only a construction, and the truth of *that* idea is only a construction, and so on forever."

"You see the point. So are you convinced skepticism is false?"

"I guess so, if we've looked at all the different forms of it."

"What about Deconstructionism?"

"What's that? I've heard of it, but I can't understand it. I can't get it in focus. It looks like a blur."

"Maybe it *is* a blur. But it says something about truth that's terribly important and importantly terrible. It claims that truth is only the hypocritical mask painted on the face of power; that truth is only whatever other people of your class or race or gender or sexual orientation or ideological group let you get away with saying. It's basically Nietzsche's shtick about everything coming down to the *will to power*."

"That IS terrible. But that doesn't mean it's not true. Racism is the gas that powers a lot of engines in our society, and that's a 'will to power'."

"But if all truth is just the will to power, *that* truth is too. So when Nietzsche or some Deconstructionist or some racist—or some anti-racist—says it to you, that can be nothing but their will to power over you. So why should you listen to them? And why should you listen to anti-racism any more than racism if they're both only the will to power?"

"No, no, that can't be. Racism can't be equal to anti-racism. It's people that are equal, not ideas."

"Gotcha! And here's another thing about racism. Deconstructionists condemn racism, but if everything comes from racism, even truth, then that's the most radical racism you can imagine."

"Suppose they say it's all a matter of gender? That it's sexism instead of racism?"

"Same argument: then that's the most radical sexism."

"And if it's all heterosexism, that's the most radical heterosexism. Then gay and straight are farther apart, not closer together."

"You're getting the gotchas."

"And if it's all economic class—that's what the Marxists say—then that's the most radical classism, the total class system. So they all end up doing exactly what they condemn. So why are they so stupid? Why don't they see that? Here we are, just two gals on a beach, and we can see the flat-out contradiction, and the great philosophers can't. That's crazy."

"Oh, I think they see it all right. They just don't care. Deconstructionists don't believe in truth, only power; that's why they want to reduce truth to power. They don't want to prove anything, only get power over you, shake you up, bug you, jerk you around, and laugh at you."

"And they call that a *philosophy*?"

"It's not a philosophy. It's a sneer. It's a snake. It's snide. It's the most dishonest and dishonorable philosophy in the history of humanity. And that's just about the nicest thing I can say about it."

"Hey, look, Mother, the sun just came out. The sky has no more clouds."

"And the emperor has no more clothes."

"So can we step up the next rung of our ladder, then, now that we've refuted skepticism?"

"We can, but I think we shouldn't, until tomorrow. I think we should step into something else first today."

"What's that?"

"Those waves. And let's just ride them instead of having a will to power over them."

"Mother, you make sense like the sea makes waves. I get the feeling there's a lot more to you than meets the eye. What's the rest of your story? What else do you make besides sense?"

"Bread. I make all kinds of bread. Do you like bread? I'll bring some to the beach tomorrow."

"It's a date."

"As for 'the rest of the story', that's always there."

"What do you mean?"

"I mean that every thing and every person is a lot more than just the little bit of it that meets the eye."

Libby's eyes involuntarily focused on Mother's ample body. Mother noticed this and smiled. "I know, I know, there's a lot of me that meets the eye—some three hundred pounds of me. But that's still only a little. We're like the ocean, I think: however big a surface you see, that's only the surface. It goes down deep and dark. And there are some really weird fish swimming around down there in all of us. But there's truth down there too, and some of it you can't get to in words but only by swimming, if you know what I mean. I think you do. You've studied psychology, you said. Well, that's swimming, no? Swimming in the psyche?"

"Yes", Libby replied. "I understand that. So let's leave the shallow little pools of words and do some swimming in the deep right now. The sun came out, and the sea is waving at us to come in."

So for the rest of the day the two of them rested from the truth made of words and entered into the truth made of water.

Dialogue Three

MEANING

The next day Mother brought to the beach three kinds of bread (plus jam and tea). One was loaded with fresh cinnamon and two kinds of big, juicy raisins; one was crusty white and tasted of extra virgin olive oil and fresh ground pepper; and the third was a multi-grain with streaks of red tomato, green basil, and mozzarella cheese running through it. Libby had never smelled or tasted such delicious bread. Mother's breads turned all other breads into sawdust and cardboard. She glanced up at the sky to see which holes from Heaven they had fallen through.

"I knew there were all kinds of breads in the world," Libby remarked, after tasting all three, "but I never knew bread could be this heavenly. You know, you could become a millionaire if you sold this stuff."

"Probably. But why should I do that? Just making it and eating it is a lot more fun. Money doesn't taste as good as bread, now, does it?"

"Mother, you make rare sense just as you make rare bread."

"Why should that be rare sense? It should be obvious, don't you think?"

"But it isn't. Plenty of people make sense about little things, like making money and predicting the weather and using computers, but not many people make sense about the big things in life, the best things in life. In fact, I wonder ..." Her voice and thought trailed off.

"You wonder if there's any truth that's like my bread. The best kind of truth: truth about the best things, the big things, the important things."

"Yes, a truth that you can bite into and eat like this bread. I thought bread like this existed only in dreams and fantasies until today. And I'm still not convinced that the kind of truth you're talking about exists outside of dreams and fantasies. I mean real, objective truth about— about the meaning of life."

"And that's exactly what we should talk about today. Okay?"

"I don't know if that *is* okay. I'm afraid we're just going to be blowing off steam if we get into something as vague as 'the meaning of life'. Maybe I'm too much of a scientist, but I want clear concepts and definite definitions first. Do you think that's wrong?"

"Not at all! I think that's right. So let's do it. Let's define what we *mean* by 'the meaning of life' before we ask whether we have any hope of *finding* it, and then let's be sure we have some hope of finding it before we set out on that road."

"Good. So what do *you* mean by 'the meaning of life'?"

"Something really simple, I think, and something that everybody means. When we say 'meaning' here, we mean 'purpose', don't we? Everything we do has a purpose, right? You eat bread because you're hungry and it tastes good and it's healthy. You put on sunblock to keep away the UV rays and sunburn. You snap that snap on your bathing suit to keep it up, so it doesn't fall down. So if each particular thing in life has a purpose, does life as a whole have a purpose or not? That's the first question about the meaning of life: Is there one? And if there is one, what is it? That's the second question."

"So you're asking what's the purpose of everything in life all together. Why it's better to live than not to live."

"Yeah."

"Well, that's the question I'm skeptical about. We can find out how to keep our bathing suits buttoned, and how to bake bread, and how to use sunblock, and we all agree about the answers to those questions because we've all found the answers. But we *don't* agree about the meaning of life. One person says it's yourself, and another person says it's God. One says it's money or pleasure or power or fame, and another says it's virtue or wisdom or beauty. So I'm thinking maybe we can't really find out what it really is, and if we can't find it out, maybe it just doesn't exist. Maybe we just make it up, like a story we decide to tell. Can you prove that that's not so?"

"Maybe, maybe not. But before you worry about *proving* whether you can find it, maybe you should first ask yourself whether you should *hope* to find it."

"Hope?"

"Yeah, hope. You hope the most for what's the most important to you, right? You hope to find a lost child more than you hope to find a lost handkerchief."

"Right."

"And this is the most important question of all, isn't it? So shouldn't you at least have a lot of hope to find the truth about it?"

"I guess we *should*, but I'm afraid most people *don't* worry about big questions like that. Only philosophers. Most people worry and hope about money and health and jobs and pains and pleasures—all those concrete particular things that loom large because they're close. Like that little piece of sharp shell I just stepped on. It's embedded in my foot, and it's bothering me now because it's stuck in the skin, so I'm trying to get it out without drawing blood. That's a little thing, I know, but to me it's such a big one right now that I can't concentrate on your words about much bigger things like the meaning of life. Do you see what I mean?"

"Of course. When you're moving down a road, the nearest telephone pole always looks the largest. *But it isn't.* It's an illusion of perspective. Objective reality doesn't match appearances. And you'd better know that, and compensate for it, or you're not going to be able to find your way home."

"But we *can* know that about telephone poles, because we can see them. But how can we know that about the meaning of life? We can't see it."

"We *don't* know the truth about telephone poles only because we see them. Just seeing them gives you illusions of perspective, remember? We know the truth about the telephone poles only because we *act*, because we experiment, we check them out. We move down the road and compare one sight with another. That's how we correct our perspective. So shouldn't we do the same with big things like the meaning of life?"

"How?"

"The same way we do it with telephone poles: by acting, by experimenting. Live one philosophy and then another, and compare them. Which works? Which makes you happy—really happy, happy in the long run? Isn't that how we know that money and fame and power aren't as important as they seem: because after you travel for a while down those roads, you're lost, you don't get home?"

"How do you know what home is?"

"Everybody knows that. It's happiness. There's no dis-agreement there. Everyone wants to be happy. We try different roads to take us there, but that's where we all want to go."

"Oh. It's that simple?"

"Yes."

"So there *is* a test."

"Yes. There is a test."

"That sounds ... scientific."

"It is. But different sciences use different instruments to make their tests. You don't use a telescope for biology or a microscope for astronomy. And you don't use either for the meaning of life."

"What do you use?"

"Your heart and your head. Those are your happiness detectors."

"Your head, that I see. But how can your heart—how can your heart *see* anything or *find* anything? It's just feel-ing, isn't it?"

"No, I think it's more than just feeling. It knows some-thing too, by intuition. You've heard that famous quote from Pascal, haven't you?—'The heart has its reasons which the reason does not know.' The heart has *reasons*, it has an eye in it. Your calculating reason isn't the only kind of reason you have."

"Now you're *not* sounding scientific. How can you use the heart to really *know* something?"

"By a kind of scientific method: by experiment, by test. Your heart is the tester. If something can't satisfy your heart's longings, deep down and long range, after you test that thing by time and experience, then that thing is not real happiness."

"Hmmm. And what are these 'longings deep down and long range' that you think everybody's heart has? Can you define them? Can you get them up into the light?"

"Certainly. Two of them are certainly happiness and meaning, or purpose."

"And pleasure too, right?"

"Yes, but that's not as deep. You can do without pleasure for long periods of time, but you can't do without meaning."

"That's true."

"Somebody said—I think it was Nietzsche, of all people—that you can endure almost any *how* if you only have a *why*. You can endure a famine of pleasure but not a famine of meaning. That's why we're not outraged by the pains of childbirth, but we're outraged when a man keeps throwing his dirty underwear on the floor."

"You got a good point there, Mother. Okay, so we long for meaning. So what? Where do you go next?"

"And we find it, in all sorts of things."

"But how do we know we can find it in *everything*, in life as a whole? Maybe we find it only in the parts. Everybody knows having a baby is meaningful, and washing clothes is meaningful, and going for a cool swim on a hot day is meaningful. But not everybody knows the answer to 'what is the meaning of life?' In fact, maybe nobody does. And I'm thinking that's because there's no scientific method for that. Because that's a philosophical question, and philosophy isn't a science. That's why it can only give you nice opinions, even profound ones, maybe, but not objective truth. It can only give you some people's opinions that other people don't believe, or stories that some people find personally meaningful but other people don't. Philosophy can't really *prove* anything. Because it doesn't use the scientific method. So it can only give you opinions. It can give you subjective truth but not objective truth."

"So you're saying that only the scientific method can give you objective truth, and philosophy doesn't use that, so it can't give you objective truth."

"Exactly. That looks like a pretty good argument to me."

"Not to me, it doesn't."

"Why not?"

"I think both of your premises are false. And I think it's easy to see that they're both false."

"How?"

"First you say that only the scientific method can give you objective truth. But that contradicts itself. Don't you see that?"

"No. How does it contradict itself?"

"That statement—that only the scientific method gives you objective truth—is that objectively true, or is that only your personal opinion or feeling?"

"It's objectively true."

"So prove it by the scientific method, please."

"I can't."

"See?"

"Oops."

"And your other premise isn't true either: that philosophy doesn't use a scientific method, that philosophy isn't a science. It *is*. It's not just nice story telling. It's a science, in all the most basic ways, even though it doesn't use telescopes or microscopes or computers."

"Why?"

"Because it's critical. It ask questions. It seeks the truth. And because it assumes a rational order in its object. And because it tries to put rational order into its thinking. For instance, it assumes rational principles like cause and effect: nothing just happens, every effect needs a sufficient cause. And above all because it tests all theories by experience, by data. In all those ways, it's a science."

"Well, then, since we human beings have been thinking more and more scientifically for the last five centuries, we should be closer to the answer than the ancients were—just like in all the other sciences."

"Do you think we are? Are we wiser? Are we happier?"

"No. We speak of 'ancient wisdom', but we don't speak much of 'modern wisdom'. We speak of 'modern science' and 'modern knowledge'. But all that progress in knowledge—it doesn't seem to have brought us progress in wisdom, if wisdom is the knowledge of the road to happiness. Because I don't think we're any happier than our ancestors, even though we know so much more. And we certainly don't all know the meaning of life clearly and confidently and certainly, as they did, or thought they did."

"I think you're right there. So what conclusion do you draw from that?"

"I'm afraid it's the one I started with: the reason we haven't found the answer, even though we've progressed so much in science, is that we *can't* find the answer by science."

"Not by biology or cosmology or medicine or math, we can't. But there are different sciences, and they use different instruments. You don't use a microscope to look for a fish, or a fishnet to look for a molecule. Why not broaden your concept of science to include philosophy?

Why not try the instrument of good rational argument—what we're trying to do right now? Are you sure we can't find answers this way? If you *were* sure of that, you wouldn't be wasting your time here with me, now, would you?"

"Okay, I guess I do have a little hope that we can find that wild goose. But not much. I think I'm in it just for the thrill of the chase. And I wouldn't call philosophy a science, as you do."

"Why not?"

"It doesn't ask scientific *questions*. Scientific questions are about facts, and we can answer those questions. Philosophical questions we can't answer because they're not about facts. They're not about objective truth. They're about subjective opinions or preferences or ideologies—those big stories that we make up ourselves about ourselves. I think they call them 'meta-narratives' nowadays. And all the answers to the really big philosophical question, the meaning of life, are just the biggest of those stories. Everybody tells her own story. Everybody makes up her own meaning. Everybody chooses her own values."

"I see. You think values aren't any kind of facts. You see a total divide between facts and values."

"Right. Isn't that what most philosophers today think too?"

"I don't know and I don't care about that, because I'm not George Gallup; I'm Maria Kirk, and I've got to do my own philosophizing. I won't let fifty-one percent of the big brains in philosophy departments do it for me. Especially because they don't usually even ask that question. They're off worrying about questions like whether we can prove we're really human beings in a real world and not just a brain in a vat in a laboratory being fed an illusion, and the whole so-called real world is just that illusion."

"Good. You're as skeptical of philosophers as I am."

"Those philosophers, anyway. Maybe they *think* they might be just brains in vats because that's all they really are: brains without hearts in the vats of academia. But not me. I'm me, here, now, with you, and we're really eating this good bread and soaking up this good sun, and *that's* the world I want to talk about and find the meaning of. What about you?"

"You got me in a 'Gotcha!' there, Mother. I'm with you. Let's philosophize about bread and sunlight, not brains and vats."

"But your notion of what philosophy is—that it's just telling stories, and making up values and meaning rather than finding the truth—that's really the same thing as saying we're only brains in vats when we philosophize. Don't you see why?"

"No, I don't."

"Well, look. These brainy philosophers say that maybe we can't really be sure we're not just brains in vats being deceived about the so-called real world, about what we think is the objective truth, about things like bread and sunlight. Right?"

"Right."

"And you're saying the same thing about meaning and value that they say about bread and sunlight. That maybe it's only our fantasy."

"Yeah, but there's a difference. We can *see* bread and sunlight. We can't see meaning and value."

"Not with the two eyes on your outside. But you have two eyes on your inside too, you know: your mind and your heart."

"Maybe they're just subjective."

"And maybe the other two are too. Maybe they're just the dream that's being fed into the brain in the vat. You see? You can't *prove* either one."

"So you're a skeptic then? You can't prove anything at all?"

"No. I think we *know* a whole lot of things that we can't *prove*."

"Like what?"

"That we exist, and that we're not brains in vats, and that bread and sunlight are real."

"But that doesn't include stuff about values."

"Yes it does. For instance, we know that a person is really more valuable than a grain of sand, and that love really is more valuable than hate, and that if every part of life has a meaning and a purpose, then life as a whole must have a meaning and a purpose too."

"I have to admit you make sense. I don't know why I find it so hard to admit your common sense."

"I think I know why. You've been educated wrong. You've been conditioned to think about reality only by the modern scientific method."

"I guess I have."

"Do you believe in God?"

"Yes, I do. I don't claim to know much about Him, or Her, or whatever God is, but I do believe in God. I was raised Southern Baptist."

"What do you believe about God?"

"Golly, I don't know. Where shall we start?"

"Let's start with this: Do you believe He really exists? Or do you think He's just a big Santa Claus that we invented?"

"I do believe He really exists. But I don't think anyone can prove that."

"Because you think that the modern scientific method is the only way to prove things, right?"

"Right."

"Do you believe in Zeus too?"

"Zeus?"

"The head honcho of the gods in ancient Athens. The cranky old graybeard with the thunderbolts who lives on top of Mount Olympus."

"No. Definitely not."

"Why not?"

"Because science has disproved him. People have climbed up Mount Olympus, and he's not there. And science has shown us where lightning bolts really come from: not from an angry old man but from electrical charges."

"So why do you still believe in God? Why isn't the God you believe in like Zeus?"

"Are you saying He is?"

"No, not at all. I just want to find out why *you* think He isn't."

"Because you can't see Him. He doesn't have a body. He doesn't have an address somewhere inside the universe, like Mount Olympus. He's the Creator."

"Good. And why can't you see the Creator?"

"For the same reason Hamlet can't see Shakespeare, as he can see his mother and the other characters in the play."

"A great analogy! So if you were Hamlet, what would you believe about Shakespeare?"

"Well, I certainly wouldn't know his name. I wouldn't know him as I know my mother."

"Why would you believe he exists?"

"Because somebody has to write the play. Plays don't just happen."

"I think that's very good reasoning. Do you see what you've been doing? You've been doing the science of philosophy. And you've told me, by that analogy, your reason for believing in God even though you don't know Him by the same method you know other things. So maybe this God stuff is not just a nice story you made up, like Santa Claus. There are no good reasons for believing in Santa Claus. But there are very good reasons for believing in God."

"Okay, let's say I accept that. How does that help us find the meaning of life?"

"If there's a God, there's got to be a meaning to life if He created it."

"I guess so. But can you prove that?"

"I think so. Look, when *we* create something, like a novel, there's always a reason, a purpose, a design, a meaning, right?"

"Right."

"Because we have a mind, right?"

"Right."

"But those waves don't have a mind, right?" (Mother pointed at the regular little waves lapping at the beach.)

"Right."

"So when millions of waves wash up on this beach for millions of years, and wash the beach away, they don't have any conscious reason or purpose or design, right?"

"Right."

"Now if there's a God, is He more like us or like waves? Does He have a mind or does He lack a mind? Is He a spirit or is He only blind matter, like salt water?"

"If He deserves the name *God*, He has to have a mind."

"Good."

"So are you trying to prove that God is the meaning of life?"

"No, I'm trying to show you that the question of the meaning of life is like the question of God. It's meaningful even though it's not empirical, even though it can't be settled by sense observation. That's why it doesn't fit the modern scientific method. It's a philosophical question, not a scientific question (if you want to use the word *science* in the narrow sense, as you do, instead of broadening it to include philosophy, as I was doing). So you have to do philosophy to answer it."

"Okay, that makes sense. But maybe it's still an unanswerable question."

"Maybe. But you have to do philosophy even to raise that question, to justify the question against your objection that it's illegitimate because it's not scientific. That's what we just finished doing: we were philosophizing about the question; we were justifying the question, not the answer."

"I guess we were. You were, anyway."

"What, you weren't here with me? I was talking to a brain in a vat, maybe?"

"No, Mother, this is the real me."

"Oh. Then I guess you were philosophizing with me."

"I guess I was."

"And was that meaningful? Or was it just nonsense?"

"It was meaningful."

"So there you are."

"Another 'Gotcha!'"

"It looks like it."

"But—but—honestly, Mother, I'm still not *sure*. I don't want to fake it just to be polite. You've opened my mind to a possibility that I've never been open to before, yes, but that's all."

"Well, then, you can at least make a meaningful Pascal's Wager about it."

"What's that?"

"Pascal said that even the agnostic who doesn't know whether God exists or not and doesn't think you can prove it or disprove it, can make a rational wager, a wise bet, and bet that He does exist, for a very good reason: because if God does exist, then the agnostic gains everything and loses nothing by believing in Him, while if God doesn't exist, the agnostic gains nothing but he doesn't lose anything either."

"So you're saying I should make a wager for God?"

"No. That may come later, but now all we're wagering about is that there is some 'meaning of life', whatever it may be."

"So you say I should make a wager about whether the meaning of life exists and whether I might be able to find it?"

"Exactly. For the very same reason Pascal gave for wagering on God. If you're right in making that wager, you lose nothing and gain everything. If you're wrong, you gain nothing and lose nothing."

"Except the time I have to take to go on that wild-goose chase."

"Right. But that's almost nothing compared with the goose, right? If you find the meaning of life, you've found something more precious than the little time it took you to find it, because you've found the meaning of *all* your times."

"Yeah . . ."

"So isn't it silly to give up hope before you even try?"

"Yes, by golly, it is. You got me there, Mother. And I'm *glad* I'm in a 'Gotcha!' now, because it's given me hope. I feel like I've just come out of a straightjacket."

"You have."

"But I'm still not sure the wild goose exists. Maybe it's a myth, like the unicorn. A lot of people think it is."

"And a lot of people tell you it isn't. They tell you they've found a unicorn. And they're not nuts."

"Like you, Mother?"

"Like me, Libby."

Libby smiled broadly. "Okay, I'll go hunting with you. Somehow I can't believe you'd lead me on a snipe hunt. I can't *prove* that, but I'll take that chance; I'll make your Pascal's Wager."

"And do you know *why* you made that choice?"

"Because it seemed rational."

"Yes, that too. But also because of the choice you made the first day we met. Because you chose to care. Because of your passion."

"I guess so. Mind you, Mother, I'm not convinced yet. But I don't want to give up before I try, because that's limp and wimpy. But I'm still in the land of Maybe. Maybe we're only dreaming a 'meaning of life', and maybe we're only dreaming God."

"And maybe we're only dreaming bread and sunlight. Maybe we're only brains in vats. But why assume that at the outset and just give up, like the two tramps in *Waiting for Godot*?"

"Because it's dogmatic to assume that there is a Godot, as they do."

"But it's just as dogmatic to assume the opposite."

"It is. So what do we do then?"

"We question both dogmas. We philosophize. We keep our minds open."

"Sounds good to me. Even though it might be just a wild-goose chase."

As soon as Libby spoke these words, one large seagull suddenly deposited itself a foot from the corner of their blanket, looked Libby straight in the eye, and let out a single very loud squawk before picking up a piece of bread and flying away.

"Is that a message from God, or what?" laughed Mother.

"If it is, it looks like God's a lot like you, Mother: He's got a weird sense of humor", Libby replied, also laughing. "But that was a seagull, not a wild goose."

"I think maybe a gull would serve as good as a goose for God, don't you think?"

"Especially when He drops a 'Gotcha!' on you. Okay, Mother, let's hunt for the meaning of life tomorrow."

"It's a date."

Dialogue Four

LOVE

A cold front had swept in during the night, bringing a short shower. The morning was cool and foggy, and the beach was wet and empty, but Mother was there. When Libby arrived, Mother suggested going indoors to talk, at "the House", as she called her ramshackle Victorian boardinghouse on the other side of the small island that was Nahant. (The island was connected to the mainland by a causeway; and the beach, over a mile long, stretched out in a half moon shape along the causeway.)

The House had its own little backyard beach of pebbles, which were muttering marine music as the waves chattered over them, making an amazing variety of sounds. Libby felt reluctant to choose between listening to Mother and listening to the symphony of the sea, but Mother solved her dilemma by plunking herself down at a table on the big backyard deck that reached out over the singing beach.

Libby met some of the other boarders in the House— Mister Mumm, with the strikingly bland face; old Lazarus, who looked and sounded like a basset hound; and Eva, a tall girl with no arms, no hair, and a seraphic smile. Diddly and Squat were there too, practicing together in a soundproofed room.*

*The reader can learn more about these and other characters in *An Ocean Full of Angels*.

Before they sat down, Mother brought out hot tea and fresh bread. At that moment, the sun began to shine through the fog, as if it had seen Mother and responded.

Libby began, "Well, Mother, I guess this is the day to hunt the unicorn: the biggest of all the big questions, What is the meaning of life? That's the next rung on the ladder logically, right?"

"Right, Libby. The logic of the ladder is in the questions."

"And here's why I'm skeptical that we can find our unicorn. I look around this House, and I see that we're surrounded by incredible variety. I just met some very strange and wonderful and unpredictable people here in this House. And now I'm listening to the music the sea is making, and I'm hearing some unpredictable sounds, sounds I never heard before, or never noticed before. The world is infinitely bigger and stranger than we ever think it is, more than we ever know."

"Oh, you're right; you're right there, girl."

"And I think our question is like that: it's just too big to catch. It's like a whale. No, it's like the whole planet. Or like the whole universe. In fact. It's bigger than the universe. The world of thought is even bigger than the world of matter. And there's a bewildering variety of answers in it. All those different cultures and times and places and peoples and religions and philosophies—I feel like a dog in a forest, as my aunt in Georgia used to say. Which tree is mine? And if I do choose one—say, I choose Solomon's answer—then I part company with Homer and Socrates and Plato and Aristotle and Confucius and Buddha and Muhammad—am I wiser than all of them? How can I know who's right? The more I study all the answers all the different thinkers have given to our question of the meaning of life, the more confused I get. So how can I make any progress by looking at more of that confusion, and adding more thinkers to my list today?"

"You probably can't", Mother replied, with an understanding nod. "But there's another way, another teacher to listen to—another *kind* of teacher."

"Who?"

"Your own heart. It's your inner teacher."

"My feelings, you mean?"

"No, your heart. The deepest thing in you. The thing that is to your soul what that blood pump in your chest is to your body. Not feelings. Feelings are *connected* to it, but they're only like nerve endings. They're external, and they're many. The heart is internal and it's one."

"I think I know what you're talking about, but it's a hard thing to set my eyes on."

"Of course it is. Your eyes look outward, and the heart is *in*. But the heart has an eye in it too. It's your inner eye. And the outer eyes depend on it, and so does your brain. If the heart didn't pump the lifeblood, the eyes wouldn't work, and neither would anything else, including the brain."

"But that's just physical."

"It's a physical *analogy* for your soul. I'm talking about your soul's heart."

"But the analogy doesn't prove anything. You haven't proved this inner teacher."

"Of course not. I'm not trying to prove it, just explain it."

"Oh, okay. But then how do I know it's there?"

"You don't have to know *how* you know something before you know it. You usually know the *how* only after you know the *what*. But you do know it. Because you talk about it. You know what I'm talking about, even though you don't know how you know it. Everybody does."

"I think you're right about that, but I'd still like some proof, or at least some reason, for believing in the heart. It's my scientific training, I guess. I just don't like to accept things without reasons, without evidence."

"Nothing wrong with that. Here's some evidence for you, then. Other people tell you something, or your culture tells you something, or your parents, or your religion tells you something; and then something else in you checks it out, and tells you either Yes or No. Maybe it says No. For instance, your culture tells you to measure a person's worth by his job, or his wealth, or by his contribution to society, or by how young and handsome and healthy he is; and your heart says No to that. You've got this inner critic, and it trumps everything else, it judges everything else. You're not just a passive construct of your society; you're a critic of it. That's why you want to change it, improve it."

"Right on, Mother. I can't deny that. Okay, so I have a heart. So how do I use it to find the meaning of life?"

"You know the answer to that one too. Listen to it, of course!"

"But when I do, I get confused. Especially when I ask it for the meaning of life."

"Yes, but when somebody speaks the magic word, the confusion suddenly goes away, like the fog went away a minute ago. And then you say, 'Of course! That's it. And I always knew it.' "

"What magic word?"

"Love. Your heart tells you that the meaning of life is love. Well, doesn't it?"

Libby was silent. "How can it be that simple?"

"I don't know *how*, but it is. Forget the *hows*. We get too hung up on *hows*. But we *know*, even without knowing how. We know what we know."

"I can't deny that. You're right. That *is* the meaning of life, and we *do* know it."

"That was easy, wasn't it? Do you want some tea now?"

"Wait a minute."

"Okay. Let's wait a minute. Let's keep listening."

"And let's listen to our brains as well as our hearts."

"Good. That's our inner teacher too. But only part of it."

"My brain—my logical mind—asks two questions about anything: define it, and prove it."

"And if you can't define it and prove it, you don't believe it?"

"Not in science, you don't."

"Is this science? What we're doing now?"

"No, this is life. But I do want to *think* about it."

"Of course."

"And I want to think logically. Do you think that's wrong?"

"Not at all; I think that's right."

"And that's what you call science in the broad sense?"

"In the broad sense, yes. You want to do the science of life. You want to do philosophy. But you don't do that on lab tables or computers or with slide rules or microscopes. It's a different kind of science. But it's logical."

"Fine. Let's do it. Let's try to define this thing called love and then let's try to prove that this thing is the meaning of life. Let's try to prove that our heart is right. But I think we're going to fail."

"And if we do fail—do we still know that our heart is right, even though we haven't proved it? Take a minute before you answer that. Be totally honest with yourself."

Libby did just that. After half a minute, she answered, "Yes, we do. I don't know how we do it, and I don't know if it's right that we do it, but we do it. We do know that love is the meaning of life. I don't know how we know that, but we know it."

"See? The *what* does come before the *how*."

"It does. It's like the basement of the building."

"So now that we've got that basement, let's see if we can build on it. Let's try to define love, and then let's see if we can prove that it's the meaning of life. We can try to build the next storey because we've got a basement. We can try to do that because we know we don't *have* to do it. We can do that without panic because we know that that precious knowledge is still there, in our heart, even if our brain can't take a photo of it. So now we can try to take that photo without worry. And I think that will give us a better chance of succeeding, because worry makes your hands shake when you hold the camera. And I think that's as true for the soul as it is for the body."

"All right, Mother. Let's try to define the love that is the meaning of life. What kind of love is it? There are all different kinds."

"I think it has to be all of them, if they're all good."

"But they're not. The love of drugs, or the love of death, for instance."

"Those are the wrong *objects* of love, but it's not wrong *to love*, is it? The love of food is the same kind of love as the love of drugs—an appetite—but it's good, because it has a good object. And the love of life is the same kind of love as the love of death—a choice, a kind of fundamental loyalty or disloyalty—but it's good, because it's a choice of the right object."

"All right, so all love is good if it has the right object. But what's the best object?"

"I think we know the answer to that question too."

"Really? I don't think we do."

"Oh, I think I can show you that we do. In fact, even the skeptics among us know that. Here, you're a skeptic, and even you know the answer to that question. In fact, you're going to tell me the answer. I'm not going to tell you. Out with it, girl! Give me what you know."

"It's the love of people, not things."

"Well, of course it is. And we all know that."

"Is that all you mean by a definition of love?"

"No, because love comes in different kinds as well as with different objects. So what kind of love of people do we mean? The love of a slave owner for his slaves? A cannibal for the tastiest people?"

"No, of course not."

"See? You know that too."

"If I know anything, I know that. My ancestors were slaves."

"So what kind of love are we looking for? What kind is the best?"

"It's unselfish love, not selfish love."

"Of course it is. See? We all know that. And what does that mean?"

"It means treating people as people, not as things. Loving them for themselves, not for you. Not *using* them."

"Another 'of course.' See? You do know that, you wise woman! We all do."

"So it means kindness."

"Yes, it does. But is that the very core of it, the essence of it?"

"I'm not sure. Maybe it is."

"If it is, then it's always got to be there. That's what an essence is. So is it ever wrong to be kind?"

"Yes. It's wrong to be kind to the druggie when he wants a handout, or to the terrorist when he wants help making a bomb. It's wrong to give someone tender love when he needs tough love."

"Yes it is. And it's wrong to be kind to your children when you see them cheating, or being cruel."

"But it's also wrong to be cruel to them."

"And is this just your strange opinion, or do we all know that?"

"We all know that, if we're sane."

"So we know what kind of love we're looking for—that it's the kind of love that is usually kind but not always, and is never cruel. Right so far?"

"Right."

"See how much you know, how much data you get from your heart? Now let's get some more. Let's find out more about the kind of love we're looking for, the kind of love that's the very essence of love and the meaning of life."

"What do you think we should look at next?"

"What do *you* think? What should we begin with?"

"With the obvious. Obviously, love has a lot to do with sex. When we think of love, we think first of in-loveness, erotic love, romantic love, love between the sexes."

"And do you think we can say the same thing about that as about kindness?"

"Remind me: What did we say about kindness?"

"That it was a very good thing, but not always."

"That fits. Sex is great, and wonderful, and amazing, but pedophilia isn't, and necrophilia isn't, and bestiality isn't."

"Why not?"

"Wrong *objects*. Just like you said before. We shouldn't have the same romantic love for children and adults, or for corpses and live bodies, or for people and animals. Even adult, live human beings are the wrong objects for it if you're married. That's called adultery. That's a kind of love, but the wrong kind. It's cheating."

"So romantic love isn't the whole meaning of life. It isn't always right. So we have to try again. What other kinds of love should we try?"

"How about friendship? That's a form of love, isn't it? Personal, intimate, trusting friendship?"

"Yes it is. But is it the very essence of love?"

"How can we find out?"

"By asking questions. Can you love other people too, even if they're not your friends?"

"Of course. Otherwise your love is terribly provincial."

"So friendship isn't the very essence of love, even though it's a very good kind."

"So how do we find the essence?"

"Let's look at what was missing when we considered friendship. You said it was too provincial, too narrow, didn't you?"

"Yes."

"And the same was true of erotic love. It's only good sometimes, not always."

"Right."

"So let's look for something more universal."

"How about 'Love your neighbor as yourself'? That expands your circle of people to love way beyond your friends. But that's not as big a turnon as erotic love or friendship. It doesn't give you the biggest rush of happiness. It's not a feeling at all."

"Maybe that's because the essence of love is not a feeling at all."

"How can it be love if it's not a feeling?"

"When you feel like punching somebody in the face and something else holds you back, is that something else a feeling?"

"Sometimes. But not always, I think."

"Might that something else be love?"

"I don't know—more likely it's guilt, I think, or fear, or some other feeling."

"Suppose you risk your life to save a stranger you've never met. Is that a kind of love?"

"Yeah."

"But it's not a feeling."

"No."

"What moves you to do it?"

"You just do it. You choose to do it, no matter what you feel."

"Exactly. It's a choice. And you make a choice with your will, right?"

"Right."

"And what is its object?"

"Other people. What they need."

"Right. Their good."

"So love would be willing the good of the other person. That sounds pretty simple."

"Then that sounds like the essence of love, doesn't it?"

"But is that *love*?"

"Why not?"

"It doesn't seem to be any kind of feeling at all."

"But we just said that the essence of love is *not* a feeling, didn't we?"

"But love without feeling—that doesn't sound very . . . it doesn't sound totally *human*. It sounds like something for angels."

"I think it's like a house." Here Mother pointed to her House, which was in the process of being repainted. Part of it was gray, part of it was purple, and part of it was scraped and not yet painted.

"How is love like a house?"

"Love usually has feelings on it, but not always, as a house usually has paint on it. Most parts of it, but sometimes not all. I'm not saying that love should be *without* feeling, just as a house shouldn't be without any paint. Love can come in many different feelings, just as a house can come in many different colors. But it's still a house even if it's not painted *any* color. So love can still be there even if it's not painted with any feeling. And it's still love, the same essence, no matter what feeling it's painted with. The feelings differ, but the love doesn't."

"Okay, I guess we've found love's essence then. But that's not saying much. What else can we say about it?"

"Good question."

"How do we answer it?"

"By asking another question. What does this love say to the other person all the time, under all the coats of feeling-paint? It always says, 'I love you.' But what *is* that, if it's not necessarily romance, or friendship, or kindness? What do you think?"

"I think it says: I love the fact that you exist, that you are real, that you are. The world is a better place, the world is a beautiful world, because you're in it."

"Wow. Look how much you know, girl! Look how wise your heart is! You should write a song about that."

At this point the door to the sound room opened, and Diddly and Squat came out, dancing to the lyrics of Elton John's "Your Song":

I hope you don't mind
I hope you don't mind
If I put down in words
How wonderful life is while you're in the world.

"I think you're a few years behind the times, Mother", laughed Libby. "It's already been done."

Diddly and Squat danced around Mother and Libby and back to their room as the song changed to Louis Armstrong's "What a Wonderful World".

"Is that a coincidence, or what?" Libby asked.

"Is anything a coincidence?" replied Mother.

"I'm convinced. I'm on board. I'm climbing the ladder. It worked. I'm thrilled. I listened to my heart, and I found the essence of love, the definition of love. That was amazing. Let's see—that was our first question. But then we had a second one—now that we have our definition of love, how can we prove that this is the meaning of life, the purpose of life? How can we do that? I've got an idea. How about if we change roles, Mother? How about if I ask the questions, and you give the answers? How about if you look into your own heart for the answer to that second question? Okay? Give me your reasons."

"All right, but they have to be yours too. You have to check them out in your own heart."

"Oh, I will."

"And they're *reasons*, but I don't think they're *proofs*. We need proofs for what we're not sure of, but I think we *are* sure of this, so I think they're just *reminders*."

"Okay, so give me your 'reminders'."

"How many would you like?"

"How many have you got?"

"As many as you want."

"You mean you can give me two if I ask for two and ten if I ask for ten?"

"I think so. They're all around us, like raindrops."

"Okay, then, just give me five."

"Sure. Here's number one: the Golden Rule. You know that, don't you?"

"Of course. 'Do unto others what you want them to do unto you.' How does that prove that love is the meaning of life?"

"What do you want most from other people? Love. When you're loved, you're happy. And everybody wants happiness. So that's how to live: give what you most want to get: love."

"But there are other things that make you happy too."

"Of course. But love trumps them all."

"Prove it."

"Okay—which would you rather be: in love in Detroit or divorced in Honolulu?"

"I get your point. So what's reminder number two?"

"Death. At death, the deepest thing in your heart comes out, doesn't it? You stop fooling yourself and playing games when you're dying, right?"

"Right."

"And what comes out at death? 'I love you.' It's the thing we say the most often, and the thing we want to say the most often, and the thing we hear the most often, and the thing we want to hear the most often, and the thing that gives us the greatest joy in that most terrible time. Isn't that true?"

"It is."

"So are you ready for my third reminder?"

"I guess so."

"It's something else we all know: that love is the secret of happiness not just for you, for individuals, but for the whole world. It's not just justice or peace but love that we need if we're going to get people together: whites and blacks, Jews and Arabs. Nothing less will do. And nothing more is needed, because once there's love, love will find a way to do everything else that needs to be done, like tearing down walls and relieving poverty and starvation and making just laws that respect everybody. We could do all that if we really, really wanted to, and we would really, really want to if we really loved those other people as we love ourselves. It's so terribly simple, it's so embarrassingly simple: we all know how to solve the world's problems, but we don't do it. It's just one thing. If we only all did this one thing—if we really, truly loved each other—this poor old world would just shake with joy and laughter from pole to pole."

"Oh, Mother, you are sooo right."

"And we all know that. And if we forget it, all our best people remind us of it: Jesus, and Martin Luther King, and Mother Teresa, and the saints of every religion in the world, and all the really great political reformers—they all say the same thing. So this is my supreme 'argument from authority'. All our authorities agree: the ones outside of us and the one inside us, our own heart."

"Not that I need any more, but give me reason number four now."

"It's a simple question: What else is there? What else would you swap love for? What's better?

"Money?" Mother suggested as an answer to her own question. "All the things money can buy? Wealth? Love is the truest wealth. If you have love in your heart, you've got real gold. The coins in your pocket are just noisemakers.

"Fame?" she continued. "Glory? Honor? Power? Hell, Hitler had all that.

"Success? Love is the ultimate success. Without that, you're a failure. Remember *Citizen Kane*.

"Control? If that's what you want, you better kill everybody else, because then you can control everything. The one thing you can't control is other people, other people's free will. And that's where love comes from. And happiness. And the meaning of life. You see, that's why love is the most precious gift: because you *can't* control it, you can't do it yourself, you can't *make* anybody love you. Even God can't do that. It's a self-contradiction.

"Physical pleasures? Nobody who's tried both ever hesitates. Nobody would give up the deep joy for the surface kicks, if they tasted both. The poor suckers who are going from one affair to another are looking for love and not finding it. If they found it, they wouldn't be so disappointed and so desperate. They wouldn't be *moving* all the time, because you don't move away from happiness, you move away from unhappiness."

"But Mother," Libby put in, "sex is pretty exciting. Ecstasy may last only a second, but it's better than boredom."

"But love isn't boring. And the deepest ecstasy in sex comes from love, from trust, from intimacy, not just from the animal rubbings and the physical pulsatings. The amazing realization that this other person loves you and trusts you so much that he holds nothing back and let you into his body and soul, that he gives up the control of his own body and put it into your hands—that's the biggest thrill, that's the ecstasy. You know what the word *ecstasy* means, literally, don't you?"

"What?"

" 'Standing outside yourself'. That's almost a definition of love, in sex and outside of it too. That's what no animal can ever get, because no animal can ever *give*, no animal can *love*."

Libby was silent, just smiling.

"There's more. You want to hear number five?"

"Yes."

"Family. Are you married?"

"No."

"Well, I am. He's gone from this world now, but I know love is the whole meaning of life because that's what made my relationship with him great and that's what makes my relationship with my children great, and those two relationships are by far the most important thing in my whole life. And love is the whole point of both of them. When there's love there, nothing in life can be better. And when there's no love there, nothing in life can be worse."

"Mother, I am totally convinced. In fact, I think my poor heart and brain can't take any more. It's on overload. My stomach is full. My soul's stomach, I mean."

"How about the other stomach? I made some great stew last night. How about going inside for a little lunch? I think we had enough mind-food today."

"Great. Will you be on the beach tomorrow?"

"If the sun is there, I'll be there. Otherwise, I'll be here. How's that?"

"Perfect. I'll be ready for the fifth rung on the ladder tomorrow. I never thought I could climb so high."

Dialogue Five

PRINCIPLES

Both the sun and Mother were on the beach the next day. Indeed, there seemed to be some mystical connection or resemblance between them, Libby thought, as she compared the sparkling sunlight with the sparkle on Mother's face, the shape of the sun with the shape of Mother's ample frame, and the sun's bursts of light with the yellow sunbursts on Mother's pleated dress. It seemed to be a good day to bring mental as well as physical things out into the brightest light.

Libby's optimism was given a shock when Mother began by saying, "You didn't put up much resistance to the first four rungs of the ladder you're climbing, but I think you probably will today. I think you'll think of this next one differently."

"Why?"

"I shouldn't have said *think* but *feel*. Your *thought* will probably climb this rung as confidently as the others, but your feeling will not come along as easily, I think."

"Again, why?"

"What did we talk about for four days? *Passion, truth, meaning,* and *love*. How do those four words make you feel? Is your inner magnet attracted or repelled by them?"

"Attracted, of course."

"And that was your spontaneous feeling about them. It was your *thinking* that was hesitant, and we coaxed it along, didn't we?"

"Yes."

"But today we're going to talk about something that will make more sense to your thinking than to your feeling. How do words like *laws* and *principles* and *rules* make you feel?"

"Bad. Cold. Negative. Suspicious. You're right. I don't like them. I like rebels; I like liberty, I like my name."

"I thought so. *Love* sounds like the sun, and *law* sounds like the moon, right? Cold and dead?"

"Right on, Mother. Love has a smile on its face, but law has a frown. Love says Yes and law says No. Love gives you personality; law gives you principles. When I hear the word *principles*, I think of P-words like *prim*, and *proper*, and *prudent*—and *prune*."

"That's the standard feeling, I think. And the standard contrast. Let's see if it makes sense, or if maybe we should be rebels against *that*."

"I see where you're going with this, Mother ..."

"I certainly hope so. I just *told* you where I'm going."

"But I'm rebelling against it already."

"I told you you would. But I didn't tell you *why* I'm going there yet. And if you haven't seen that yet, you can't rebel against that yet, can you?"

"Yes I can. If I don't like the house at the end of the road, I won't like the road."

"Did you like my House, yesterday?"

"Yes. A lot."

"Why? Because you visited. You tried it."

"Right."

"You might even come to live there some day."

"Are you inviting me?"

"Well, sure, if you want to. But you see, you don't know whether you like it until you try it. You can't tell whether the dress fits until you try it on."

"So you want me to try on a new dress called 'law-and-principle' today to see how it fits over the 'love' underwear I agreed to wear yesterday."

"That's a good way of putting it, yes."

"I'll tell you what that looks like to me. It looks like asking me to try on the moon to cover the sun."

"I know that's the way you see it, but ask yourself: *Why* do you see it that way?"

"Because love is expressive and law is repressive. Love is a Yes and law is a No."

"To what?"

"To anything."

"And what thing do you think of first when you say that?"

"Sex, I guess."

"Is that just a guess, or is that what you know?"

"I know it, I guess. Oops—that's a contradiction, isn't it?"

"I won't push that. Sometimes a guess is enough. Okay, let's look at sex. Love of your guy says: 'Yes, have sex with him, because of love.' And lack of love for some other guy says: 'No, don't have sex with him, because you don't love him.' Right?"

"Right. Exactly."

"So you don't need any law there, right?"

"Right."

"Now suppose you're in love with a nasty bastard who's abusing you."

"I'm not."

"Some women are. Imagine you're one of them."

"I can't imagine myself doing that."

"Really? So you can't have any sympathy for those women?"

"Of course I can. I've helped dozens of them when I was a social worker."

"Then you *can* imagine it. Because if you can't even *imagine* it, you can't sympathize with them either, can you?"

"Okay, so I can *imagine* it."

"Or imagine you're in love with a goat."

"Sexually, you mean?"

"Yes."

"Why would you want me to imagine something that stupid?"

"To make a point. It's a thought experiment."

"Okay, so I got this hotty goat. So what now?"

"Is it good for you, is it wise for you, is it happy for you to just follow love? Or do you need some law, some principle, something to say No sometimes? Something to correct you, and protect you against harming yourself?"

"Oh, of course I need that. The more stupid I am, the more I need it."

"Okay, let's call what you need law. You need law— why? For love, right? To straighten out love. To get your love life in order. To make your love better. Not to abolish it."

"Right."

"So law should be love's servant, not love's master. Love's ally, not love's enemy, right?"

"Right. Love is the purpose of law."

"Next question: If that's law's end, is it also its beginning?"

"What do you mean, 'beginning'?"

"Where does this wise and helpful law come from? Does it come from outside love, or does it come from inside love? Is it like a barnacle or like a blossom?"

"Sometimes it's a barnacle. Like the stupid state laws that stopped me from helping people in distress last year. That's why I quit. Sometimes laws can be repressive; I know that from experience."

"Yes, they can. But that very judgment—that some laws are bad because they're repressive instead of progressive—that assumes a standard to judge laws by, doesn't it?"

"Yes."

"And isn't that standard the very nature of the thing the law is supposed to help? Which in your case was people?"

"Yes."

"So the same thing must be true for human love. The nature of human love isn't perfected by abuse, or bestiality; that's why law says no to them. It's the natural law, the law of the nature of love itself. But bad laws are unnatural: not only artificial but harmful, repressive. Right?"

"Okay. Good laws are blossoms; bad laws are barnacles."

"So good laws come from inside love, from love itself. *Love* wants these laws, needs these laws, as soldiers need shields: as defensive weapons, when love is threatened. Which is pretty much in our world, I think."

"I agree."

"So *that's* the kind of law I'm talking about today."

"Okay, that's different. But love doesn't need any laws to protect it unless it's being threatened."

"And when *isn't* it being threatened in this poor old world? Have you ever seen another world, a Garden of Eden?"

"No. I get your point."

"But I don't think that's the only reason for laws: protection, defense. Doesn't everything in nature have its own natural laws even when it's not being threatened? Like gravity for matter, and photosynthesis for plants, and evaporation for liquids?"

"I see what you mean. Of course."

"Then you were wrong to think of law as the natural enemy of love."

"But most people do. That's the standard view. And that's got to make some sense too, or it would never have become the standard view. There's got to be some truth to it."

"Sure. It's true of bad laws, unnatural laws. But not good ones, not natural ones."

"I guess that's right."

"Let's test the guess. Let's apply 'the standard view' to anything real, any other part of life. Like social work, or counseling, or investments, or travel, or translating languages, or singing. We don't have to go into detail, I think. Isn't it plain as pie that if you do any of those things without knowing the natural laws of the thing and without respecting those laws, that you'll fail? That you'll flop like a dead fish?"

"Yes."

"So love alone isn't enough. You need law too, and you need to *know* the laws, and you need to *obey* them."

"If they're natural laws, yes."

"Isn't that true of *everything* in life?"

"Yes, I guess it is."

"Well, *I* don't think it is. Not quite. I think you said Yes too fast there, girl."

"Where isn't it true?"

"Dreams. Fantasies. Fictions. There, you make whatever laws you like. You want to write a story about life on a planet without disease or death, or without light or gravity, you can do it if you've got enough imagination. But if you're dealing with anything real, you need to know the real laws of the thing."

"You're right."

"So now let's apply that to love. If love is only a dream and a fantasy, if love is only a private feeling, if love is only subjective, then we don't need to look for its laws. But if it's something real, then we need to know its real laws. Isn't that the logical conclusion we have to draw?"

"It is."

"So if we're sure of that, what's the next question?"

"What *are* those laws and principles, of course."

"Of course. Once you know they exist, you want to know what they are."

"And how do we find them?"

"What do *you* think?"

"By experience, and experiment. By living. We see what works and what doesn't."

"True. We do. But that's learning the hard way, isn't it?"

"Yes. But it's the only way."

"Is it? There's an old saying that goes, 'Only fools learn by experience.' Do you have to put your finger in the fire and burn your skin to learn that fire burns?"

"Not always."

"So sometimes there's another way to learn besides the hard way. There's the easy way."

"So what's the easy way to learn the laws of love?"

"Here's another word you won't like. It's called *authority*."

"You're right: I don't like that word."

"What do you think it means?"

"It means, 'Do this because I say so, and I'm the boss.' It means, 'Might makes right.' "

"No it doesn't. It means, 'Right makes might.' It means, 'Right works.' Authority means having the *right*, not having the *might*. Hitler had the might to kill six million Jews, but he didn't have the right to do it; he didn't have the authority to do it. The bastard who abuses his girlfriend has the might to do it, but he doesn't have the authority to do it. I'm twice as big as you, and I have the power to hold you down and handcuff you and imprison you in my House if I wanted to. But I have no authority to do that. You're not my prisoner, and I'm not a cop."

"Okay, so authority is 'right', not 'might'. So what?"

"So authority is one way to learn, and experience is the other. Authority is the easy way, and experience is the hard way."

"So what's the authority here? What's the authority for the laws of love? Are you talking about God? About religion?"

"No, not yet. Just morality."

"Which morality? There are plenty of different moralities."

"No there aren't. There's only one, because there's only one human nature. I mean the morality everybody knows by nature, by natural conscience, innately."

"Oh. I thought you were talking about something like the Ten Commandments."

"I *am* talking about the Ten Commandments."

"But that's just one particular set of rules."

"No it's not. Everybody knows them. Every religion and every culture and every society has some version of them. Did you ever hear of a society that believed that murder and adultery and lying and stealing and selfishness were *good*, and respecting your parents and reverence for God were *evil*?"

"Well, no. But religion is a matter of faith, and there are dozens of different religions, and ..."

"I'm not talking about religions; I'm talking about morality. Don't you think nonreligious people know morality too?"

"Well, sure they do."

"So we're not talking about religious faith here, which is what *some* people *believe*. We're talking about morality, which is what *all* people *know*."

"Fine. So we all know some basic moral principles. How does that apply to love?"

"That's what those principles *are*: the principles of love!"

"Well, I guess that makes sense: if they're the principles for living your whole life, then they must apply to love too ..."

"No, not 'love *too*', as an afterthought. That's their whole point. The Commandments are for love, and love is for life; that's why the Commandments are for life. They describe love. *Love* does not kill, *love* does not steal, *love* does not bear false witness, *love* does not commit adultery."

"But love *does* commit adultery. It happens all the time!"

"Not real love. Not unadulterated love."

"Oh. Gotcha."

"And love worships, and love takes a Sabbath, and love respects parents, and love doesn't worship idols, or fake gods, *any* kind of fake gods. Love is not fake, love is authentic, love is true, love is real. *That's* what the Commandments are all about."

"I never looked at it that way."

"You're looking at it that way now."

"And I like the way it looks. I might actually come to love those old laws if I look at them this way."

"Why? Because you love love. Because whatever you love, you love the natural laws of that thing, and the Commandments are the natural laws of love, the laws of the nature of love."

"I see. That's why today naturally follows from yesterday, like rungs on the same ladder, right?"

"Exactly. Yesterday we found that love was the meaning of life, the purpose of life, the best thing in life. So we fell in love with love, and that's why we'd be right today to fall in love with the laws of love."

"That makes sense, at least in theory. But I'm a practical girl: Is that how it has to work out in practice, in life, with real, flawed people?"

"You know it does. You know that from your experience. If a guy really loves a girl, he'll want to know her nature, the laws of her nature, everything about her, who she really is, what makes her tick. But if he only wants to use her, if he only wants her for his own kicks, he couldn't care less about why she loves olives so much."

"Okay, so I guess the war between love and law is ended. We have peace now."

"No, we still have war."

"We do? Why?"

"We have a different war now: the war between good law and bad law, between natural law and unnatural law."

"Oh. Gotcha! That explains why I wasn't wrong to be skeptical of all those artificial, arbitrary rules and regulations."

"Exactly. They weren't natural, so they weren't real. They weren't the laws of the reality of the thing. But natural laws are, because they come from the real thing, not from something else, not from some person's arbitrary will and personal desires. They're like the laws of physics, not like the laws of Massachusetts."

"I see your point. It would be a pretty pitiful universe if it had to run by the laws of Massachusetts."

"Well, that was a happy 'Gotcha!'"

"Where do we go from here?"

"Let's wait till tomorrow to find out."

Dialogue Six

GOD

The next day was hot and overcast. The light seemed to be coming from all quarters at once: sand and sea, earth and sky, left and right. Though some complained of the heat, Libby and Mother both thought it a pleasure, not a pain, because it gave a keen edge to their appreciation of the refreshing cold of the water.

Mother and Libby did not speak about their "ladder" for the first hour or so, but were content in the healing seawater, which was being magically troubled by small angels. Mother suspected that Libby was reluctant to explore the ladder's next step, and so when they had dried themselves off and plunked themselves down on Mother's bright red beach blanket, she asked, frankly, "Are you in the mood for a climb on our ladder, or do you just want to 'lizard around' today?" (This was Mother's phrase for relaxing in the heat.)

"Not sure", Libby replied, with equal frankness.

"And why is that, pray tell?"

Libby had not heard that antique expression for years, and smiled a little as she replied, "I'm afraid of running into an old friend today—or an old enemy—someone who's been a little bit of both to me."

"I think I know Him", Mother replied. "And I think I understand how you feel about Him. It's God, isn't it?"

"Yes", said Libby, surprised that her camouflage had been so transparent. "So far, we weren't talking about God. We were talking about us, and about human love. And we were going along swimmingly, I thought. And I want to keep swimming in that direction, in that comfortable shallow water. I don't want to change direction and head out to sea where the water is over my head, because I'm not that good a swimmer."

"I understand you, girl. You're afraid I'm getting ready to bat you on the head with a Bible."

"Not literally, but . . . something like that. I've got mixed feelings about The Big Guy Upstairs, and I hoped we wouldn't bump into Him on the ladder. But I suspected all along that that's where the ladder was going. It's going *up*, after all. That's why I was a little reluctant to start the first step, I guess. I was afraid you'd bring God in on one of the steps, and now I suspect it's probably this one."

"Well, thanks for being so frank with me, girl! But believe me, I do understand how you're feeling, even though I don't feel that way myself. I suspect most of us feel the way you do sometimes, but we aren't honest enough to admit it. When we're doing our own thing and doing okay, we don't like interference from The Big Guy Upstairs any more than we like it from the little guys down here."

"So we *don't* have to bump into *Him* today? You weren't setting me up?"

"Well, I wasn't planning a Bible bashing. And I wasn't planning to write an invitation letter to Heaven to come and crash our little party. But I *was* planning on following our ladder *wherever* it leads. Weren't you?"

"Yes. That's what I decided to do the day I put my foot on the first rung. But I'm hoping it's really a ladder and not an escalator. You *can't* get off an escalator once you put your foot on the first step. But you have to *choose* to climb each step of the ladder."

"Oh, it's a ladder, all right, because it's a *human* journey, and therefore it has to be a free one. I'm not planning to change your name, Libby."

"I believe you. So let's stay with love for a while, shall we? I'd rather explore that than anything else."

"What if God turns out *not* to be 'anything else'?"

"What exactly do you mean by that?"

"I mean, will you go wherever love takes you?"

"Absolutely."

"Even if it takes you up to The Big Guy?"

"Hmmm. Is that a 'Gotcha!'?"

"I didn't mean it to be. I'm just trying to x-ray your insides now, not arguing with you."

"Then yes, I'll give love a blank check. But not God. Look, Mother, I don't want to shock you, but I have to tell you something about myself. *Dog* is *God* spelled backward, and I love God backward more than forward. I love dogs more than I love God. I had a dog for ten years—Sammy—and he gave me more love than any human being I ever knew. He was always there for me, and he'd forgive me when I was nasty, and he'd be so happy when I was nice, and he just spilled over with happiness whenever I came home. He gave me more love than anybody ever gave me, 'cept my mama. He died last month, and I cried for a week over him. But if I read a headline that said, 'God is dead', I wouldn't cry. I wouldn't care as much about that as I cared about my Sammy."

"I hear you, girl. I think a lot of people feel that way. But suppose Sammy was just channeling God, mediating

God? Suppose his love was just a tiny reflection of God? Something like the back side of God, God backward. Maybe God put that pun in our language."

Libby laughed. "Can a pun be a prophet?"

"Why not? Why wouldn't God have a sense of humor? How could He be God if He lacked something good that we had?"

"But if He's so good, why did Sammy give me more happiness than He did?"

"Maybe he didn't. Maybe Sammy was only a reflection of His happiness, like that little patch of sunlight there on your leg is a reflection of the sun."

"I see where you're going with this, Mother, and I think I just can't go there. Love, yes, religion, no. And that's not because I don't take love seriously, but because I do. And I know it's not going to lead me to anything or anybody who represses it, or ignores it, or pours cold water on it."

"And that's how you see The Big Guy?"

"Yeah."

"Maybe you need to meet another one. Maybe yours isn't the only one."

"Oh. Well, I have to admit that that's a refreshing thought. Maybe the other one isn't so big. And maybe He's not a guy."

"Well, if He's *God*, He's not a batch of molecules in space, so He's *not* big. And He's not small either, for the very same reason. And if He's God, He's not a guy either. And He's not a girl either, for the very same reason."

"You mean because He's the *Creator* of big things and little things and guys and girls—and dogs too, right?"

"Well, yes, but I thought you didn't want to do theology today. I thought you wanted to explore love more."

"I do, I do. But if 'God is love' ..."

"Go on. Finish the thought."

". . . then there might be a real connection."

"Yes, I would think 'is' would be a pretty strong 'connection'. But I think you're climbing backward now. You're climbing down instead of up."

"What do you mean by that?"

"I mean that you start from your idea of God, then you wonder whether God is love or whether God is The Big Guy Upstairs who seems to be the enemy of love. You're working from the top down, from God to human love. You're starting with theology. I thought we weren't doing that. I thought we were climbing this ladder from the bottom up. And if we are, then the question is not whether God is a lover, but whether love is divine."

"You mean maybe 'God is love' can be turned around, like an equation, into 'Love is God'?"

"No, not quite. It doesn't work that way. It's not like math. The two equations don't mean the same thing. I don't think there's anything wrong with the first one—'God is love'—but I think there *is* something wrong with the second one—'Love is God.' "

"Why?"

" 'God is love' means 'This God you already know is bigger than you know. He's love. He's pure love.' That's news. Not everybody who believes in God knows that."

"That's for sure."

"But 'Love is God' means 'This love you already know is bigger than you know'—and *that's* true, all right—'and it's so big that it's not just *from* God but it *is* God. Search no more; that's all God is, human love. There's no more in God than that.' And maybe that's *not* all right. Do you see the difference?"

"Yes."

"And do you see what's wrong with the second formula?"

"For religious believers, yes. If that formula is true, then there is no Big Guy Up There any more, just love down here. So that would be an insult to religion, I guess. But that doesn't bother me. I'm not an atheist, but I'm skeptical of religion. I drink my coffee without cream and sugar, and I'll take my God without religion, thank you."

"But that's what it *means*: the word *religion* means 'relationship'—relationship with God."

"But I don't believe in any of the little boxes the churches put Him into. I don't think anybody can ever catch Him. Nobody *has* Him. He's like the light."

"Oh, I think you're right there—*sooo* right. But do you know who teaches you that?"

"The poets? The mystics?"

"The churches. Some of them, anyway."

"Oh. Well, good for them, then."

"So maybe you should listen to them."

"But they contradict each other. So they can't all be right. Which one has it right? How do we know? I'm skeptical of anybody's claim to answer *that* question."

"But we're not talking about that question now."

"But we will soon, right? Like tomorrow? Your ladder is aimed *somewhere*."

"Every ladder is. But we have to follow it, step by step, not steer it. We have to follow what we've already found. We can climb up only on the rungs we've already climbed up on. We've checked out those rungs already, and they'll hold us. But we haven't checked out any other ones yet. We have to do it step by step. One thing at a time, okay?"

"Okay. So where are we now?"

"We're asking whether love leads to God or not. If not, not. We don't go there. And if so, then we do go there. That's why we were looking at the relationship between love and God. And we were checking out the formula that says that love is God. And I was giving you my reasons for being skeptical of that formula."

"You said it insults religion. But I don't give a damn about that."

"No, I didn't say it insulted religion. You did. My problem with the formula is not that it's an insult to religion, or even to God, but that it's an insult to love. And love is the one thing we've found so far that we know we'd better not be insulting and cutting down to size."

"How is it an insult to love? It sounds like the biggest compliment you could possibly pay to love, to say that it's God."

"It's cutting love down to too small a size."

"But it seems to be just the opposite: making it as big as anything can be."

"Not really. Because what that formula means is that the love we already know, love from human beings, is God and there's nothing more. There is no God above human love, and therefore *no love above human love*. It says that love is only human, that love isn't Godlike because there is no God."

"I follow that."

"And do you see why that's an insult to love? Are you looking with love's eyes now, and do you see what love sees?"

"You mean love has to be more real than just the little bits of it that we have."

"Exactly. And that was exactly the insight you had a minute ago about God. No little boxes."

"It is, isn't it? I guess that's a 'Gotcha!'"

"That's why we should say, 'Love is *Godlike*', instead of saying, 'Love is God.'"

"Okay, fine, but—all this talk about the right formula, and reversing the formula, and which term is the subject and which one is the predicate—that talk about formulas and terms sounds awfully abstract. Can you make it more concrete?"

"I'll try. Let's see ..." Mother paused to think, and at that very moment the sun suddenly shone through the cloud cover.

"There it is!" said Libby. "Like a sentence in the sky. Hey! The Guy Upstairs just left a fingerprint. 'Love is like sunlight, and God is like the sun'—that's what you're trying to say, Mother, right? He just said it for you."

Mother smiled, and muttered, "I love it when He does stuff like that. Yes, that's it. All this sunlight comes from the sun, whether we see it or not. We can trace all the sunlight back up into the sun. So maybe we can trace all the love light, all the little rays of love we know, back to the God who's Absolute Love. Maybe that's where it all comes from."

"I guess that's the kind of God-question I can live with", Libby said. "That's not about formulas. It's about love, and that's something we can experience. I was afraid we were going to get off into the abstract question."

"What abstract question?"

"You know, the philosophical question, 'Does God exist?'"

"And why don't you like that question?"

"That's about existence, about reality, but not about love. That's the question of 'How big is reality? Does it include a God?' But we're going into the love-question, the question lovers ask: 'How big is love? Does it go all the way up? Is it bigger than we are?' That's our question now isn't it? Is love smaller than life or is it larger than life?"

"Yes. And is it bigger than *death*?" Mother added. "Or does it die when we die?"

"So when I ask that question, I'm climbing the next rung of the ladder."

"Yes you are, girl."

"Well, let's do it."

"Let's."

"But how?"

"Why, with the same muscles you used to climb the other rungs of the same ladder, of course: with your head *and* with your heart. You don't want to leave your head behind when you climb the ladder, do you?"

Libby smiled. "No. I'm glad that's not an either-or. I'd hate to leave either my heart or my head behind on the sand like a lost beach ball."

"You'd look pretty funny missing either one of them when you got to the top—which I think you'd never do anyway without both of them. You use two lungs to breathe, and two eyes to see, and two legs to climb. You use your heart-leg and your head-leg."

"I'm with you there. So let's climb."

"Okay. Then let's consult our two legs. Tell me first what your heart says about love when you ask it how big love is, how high it goes. Does it say that love dies when you die? Is it smaller than you are, or bigger? Is it 'bigger than both of us', like the old movies say?"

"It has to be. Maybe not the silly sentimental kind of love that those old movies are talking about—Cupid shooting his arrows and all that stuff—but some kind of love, the heart of love, the essence of love—that has to be bigger and stronger than us."

"So does that come *out of* your heart or does it come *into* your heart?"

"What do you mean?"

"Can anything bigger than your heart come out of it?"

"That doesn't sound logical. The effect can't be greater than the cause."

"So when you look at how big love is, are you bigger than it or is it bigger than you?"

"I just admitted that it's bigger than we are—the old movie cliché is true."

"So you don't make it so much as it makes you. So it's not like a flashlight but like the sunlight."

"Yeah."

"And if there's a sunlight, there's a sun."

"Oh. I guess that does prove the existence of God."

"Let's look at it again, to be sure. Let's look at our data."

"What data?"

"Our experience, of course. Where else could we start?"

"You mean like … the creation proves the Creator, and design proves a designer, and motion proves a first mover? Those old philosophy proofs?"

"We could go into that if we want to, but I was looking at the other side of our experience, the inside. It gives us inside information. That's a richer database, I think, and I think it will lead to a richer conclusion too."

"What do you mean by 'a richer conclusion'?"

"Well, the motion argument may lead to a First Mover, and the design argument may lead to a First Designer, and that's all pretty abstract. But the argument from love may lead to a First Lover. A thicker notion of God."

"Okay. I'm on board with that."

"So let's look at your experience of love. Do you experience it as you experience sunlight? Does it feel like light from a higher source, that just keeps coming, more and more of it, in an unlimited supply, like that sun? Or does it feel only like the blood in your circulatory system: a limited amount, and inside you from the start instead of coming onto you from something else, like light? All that your physical heart does is to *pump* the blood that's already in you. But your eyes don't do that to light. They receive it from outside, from on high. So what does love look like? Like blood or like sunlight?"

"If you use those analogies, it's got to be more like sunlight than like blood. I don't know how I know that, but I know it. *Some* kind of love has to be that. *Something* has to be stronger than death. Maybe some other kinds of love aren't. They can be like the blood. But one kind of love, at least, has to be like the sunlight. Because *something* has to be stronger than death, and I hope with all my heart that that something is love."

Mother said nothing, but just smiled, as the sun was now doing in the sky.

Libby went on, in a more reflective tone: "I seem to have discovered a kind of fiery little rabbi in my heart. Something like a little sun. It just *demands* that love go all the way up. And ... and that little sun is in my head too, because it says that all this is *logical*. If we were right yesterday when we said that love is the meaning of life, then, if we're logical, we have to say that love is stronger than death, and bigger than death, and not just one of those little parts of life that death kills in the end."

Mother just nodded.

"But that's not a proof", Libby admitted. "I'm afraid I'm not saying it the way the philosophers would say it."

"They're not here now to grade you, are they?"

"No."

"But your own heart and head are."

"Yes."

"And they're not flunking you, are they?"

"No. But ... it's logical, but it's not a *proof*."

"When a scientist wants to marry an equation, she needs a proof. When Juliet wants to marry Romeo, does she need a *proof*?"

"No."

"What does she need?"

"Courage."

"Is she wrong, then, to say Yes?"

"No."

"Even without being able to *prove* that she's not wrong?"

"She's not wrong. She *knows*. She just knows."

"And so do you."

"But do we have to call that 'God'? I want to open my door to *that*, but I think I want to keep a lock in place to God."

"You mean 'The Big Guy Upstairs'."

"Yeah."

"Maybe that's not God. Maybe that's the projection of your own fears, like an echo in a canyon."

"But maybe the love-God is only the projection of my wishes. How do I know which is the real thing and which is the projection?"

"Ask your two prophets. Ask your head: Which God is bigger than you are and which one is smaller? Then ask your heart the same question. And if you get the same answer from both ..."

"Then I put my hand out and invite Him in. Like Juliet."

"Like Juliet."

"But ..." Libby looked like a skydiver without a parachute.

"Finish the thought, girl. I'm here. I'm a big airport; you can land your plane."

"But if I invite Him in, *anything* can happen. I'm not in control any more. No guarantees."

"Right. There are no guarantees."

"I don't like that!"

"Neither do I. And that tells us a lot about our feelings, but it doesn't tell us a lot about the real world, does it?"

"But why does life have to be that way?"

"Because of what we discovered yesterday: because it's about love, not math. And love is a leap of faith, not an equation."

"It's scary."

"Climbing usually does get scary at some point on the ladder."

"So my choice to climb or not to climb—that's still my free choice, isn't it?"

"Of course it is."

"And that choice isn't going to be decided by a proof."

"That's what it looks like."

"So it's going to have to be made by my heart."

"Yes."

"But if my heart can't just follow my head, what *is* going to sway my heart?"

"Your courage." Mother looked Libby straight in the eye.

Libby smiled ruefully. "Why does love need so much courage?"

"For the same reason a little kid needs courage to sleep in the dark: he's afraid of the boogeyman. Because some idiot told him that stupid story about the boogeyman and scared him."

"And that little kid is me?"

"I think so. You're afraid of The Big Guy Upstairs. That's your boogeyman. And you're afraid because some idiot told you some stupid story about that boogeyman, and scared you."

"What story?"

"I don't know what they told you, but I know what they *didn't* tell you. They didn't tell you that He was love. They told you that He *wasn't* love. They told you that love doesn't go all the way up. They told you this not in so many words, of course, and probably more by actions than by words, but they told you that love is just down here, under the clouds; so when you climb up high enough, beyond the clouds, to places you can't see from down here, you won't find love but something else."

"Yeah, that's the message I got, anyway. But how do I *know* that's not true?"

"By using your head and your heart."

"My heart doesn't *want* that to be true, but my head can't *prove* it's not true."

"You can't prove it, but you can believe it. And your head can give you good reasons to believe."

"Like what?"

"Like what we both just said: love without God is like sunlight without the sun."

"Gotcha!" Libby nodded decisively.

"I think I just saw your foot step up one rung."

"It did. So where do we go next? What comes tomorrow?"

"Let's let tomorrow worry about tomorrow."

Dialogue Seven

JEWS

The next day the weather was perfect but hot; and the beach was crowded with a microcosm of global humanity, male and female, old and young, black and white. In the heat and the crowding, a loud argument broke out between two groups of young men, not far from Mother's blanket. Libby commented, "Sorta sounds like the history of religions."

"Funny you should say that", Mother answered. "Because that's the next problem we ought to face today. We got as far as God yesterday, but we didn't pin Him down to any religion—and I don't think we should, but I think we should look at the embarrassing fact that all the different religions seem to contradict each other."

"Maybe they don't. Not about the most important thing. Not about love and compassion and mercy and forgiveness and unselfishness. Don't they all teach some version of what we just found out was the meaning of life yesterday?"

"Yes, but you're forgetting something. That wasn't yesterday. It was the day before yesterday. You're forgetting yesterday. Yesterday we talked about God. The religions do contradict each other about God."

"But not about love."

"Maybe a little bit about love too, as well as a lot about God. And if love is so important, then even if they contradict themselves only a little bit about love, it becomes very important which version of it is right. Because it's about the most important thing in the world, isn't it?"

"I guess it does matter. It's certainly more important than theologies and creeds and institutions and codes and laws and different ways of worship, anyway. Those all look like little boxes to me, little systems, little maps. You can't put God into systems or boxes or maps."

"Of course you can't. But God is what all those things are *about*. Those different religions are different road maps to get to God, road maps for the relationship with God— the God we admitted yesterday was the most important thing of all, the God who is love and who is the meaning of life. If the differences between the religions are about *that*, then if we ignore those differences, we're saying we don't really care about getting *that* right. And that means we don't really care about *that*."

"Okay, so it's for the sake of *that* that we have to go into the different religions' claims about God, I guess. I'm not happy doing that, but I can't refute your logic, Mother."

"It's not *my* logic. It's the logic of the argument—no, more, it's the logic of reality."

"I guess I can't argue with reality. Whenever I bump up against it, skin comes off my nose, not off reality. Okay, so let's try to climb another rung on our ladder and try to get a better look at whoever's on top of it."

"Oh, I don't think *that* will work."

"Neither do I. But why don't you?"

"That would be like Hamlet trying to get to Shakespeare."

"That's what I say too, Mother. Our cars don't have big enough fuel tanks, and Heaven doesn't appear on our road maps. It's like what the Vermont farmer said to the New Yorker who asked him for directions: 'Ya can't get there from here.' You sound refreshingly agnostic, Mother. I agree with you. I've always suspected that any God you *could* get to from here would have to be a figment of your imagination. That's why I always thought religion was a kind of patronizing pat on the head and a 'Yes, Virginia, there is a Santa Claus.' Or else fundamentalist Bible-bashing, at the other end of the spectrum. So what do we turn to next if religion is hopeless?"

"Not so fast!"

"Oh—oh. Do I hear sleigh bells on the roof? Or is it the sound of Bibles being thrown through the air?"

"We haven't *looked* yet. How can we say No before we look? Do you say Yes before you look?"

"Of course not."

"So do you say No before you look?"

"I guess not, not if I'm going to be fair. But we can't look at all of the world's religions in one conversation, even if they do all say pretty much the same thing."

"But they don't. One is different."

"They're *all* different. Otherwise there wouldn't be more than one."

"But one is different even in the way it's different. It's *radically* different. It's a different *kind* of religion."

"How can any religion be a different *kind* of religion? There's just one religious mountain, and many paths up the same mountain. Why should one path be better than all the others if we made them all?"

"Because maybe we didn't make them all. Maybe God made one of them. Maybe He didn't just sit there waiting for us to come up, maybe He came down. Maybe He revealed Himself. Maybe there's a divine revelation."

"Isn't *everything* a divine revelation, if there's just one God? The sunlight, and dogs, and human love—isn't that all God revealing Himself, if He created it all? Maybe once upon a time some great mystic like Buddha or some great philosopher like Confucius figured out a little more of that revelation than anybody else, so if we're open-minded, we should just take each of these private geniuses seriously, and join them as best we can, each of us in her own way, like making a string of beads to wear. But that still doesn't make one public religion for everybody."

"But suppose this God revealed Himself publicly, to a whole people, not just privately, to an individual mystic. Suppose *that's* where we have to look for this one path down that God made Himself: outside instead of inside. And then, when we do look outside, in history, we do find one such people, the most remarkable people in history, one of the smallest and weakest of peoples but one that survived for four thousand years even though everybody was always hating them and trying to wipe them out. And yet half of what has survived in Western civilization came from them, including the best moral code in the history of the world, the one the world still lives by, as well as the theology half the world believes."

"Oh. You're Jewish, aren't you?"

"Yes, but so are you, if you're a Christian."

"What do you mean by that?"

"That you learned who God is from us Jews. You learned that He's One, and a Person, and the Creator, and eternal, and perfect, and faithful, and trustable, and moral, and loving. You didn't learn that from the Greeks or the Romans or the Egyptians or the Sumerians. And it was from the Jews that you also learned what God wants *from us*: I mean the Law, the Ten Commandments—which Jesus summarized as nothing but love. So we're still talking about love today."

"But *everybody* knows God and the Ten Commandments now, not just the Jews."

"Half the world knows it, yes. Two billion Christians and one billion Muslims, the world's two largest religions. But where did they learn it? From the Jews, the world's smallest major religion. That's just a historical fact."

"And how is this such a radically different *kind* of religion, a different *kind* of road up the mountain?"

"It's not a road up the mountain—it's a road down. God made it, not man. And it's public, not private. It's a public revelation from the top down, not a private mystical experience from the bottom up."

"But even if it *is* a road down and not just a road up, the message that comes down this road is pretty much the same message as the one that comes from all the other roads, the roads that go up instead of down, the religions you say are only human. We all know how we ought to live. We all know we shouldn't be selfish little pigs."

"We all know the moral message, yes, but we don't all know the message about God. We didn't have to get into the question of 'Which religion?' when we talked about love, because religions are very similar there because they all demand that we overcome our primary instinct, selfishness. But we do have to get into the question of 'Which religion?' when we talk about God, because the different religions are *not* similar there. Their message about God *is* different. Very different."

"How?"

"For one thing, the Jewish God is the only Creator God."

"No it isn't. Every religion and mythology in the world has its creation stories."

"No, they're not creation stories, they're formation stories. Their gods just brought order out of chaos. This God brought being out of nothing. That's what *creation* means. There's even a separate word for it in Hebrew—*bara'*—that doesn't exist in any other language. It's a verb in Hebrew that never has anyone but God as its subject. No matter how 'creative' we are, we can't really create. We can only make and form and shape. We can make new forms, but God makes new matter. Nobody else in all of human history anywhere in the world ever got that idea into their head unless they learned it from us: that God created the whole universe, created matter and time and space itself, out of nothing, not just shaped it out of something that was already there."

"Okay, so maybe you have the best theology. But everybody has morality."

"But nobody else's morality goes all the way up into their theology! That's why theology is so important; that's why which God you believe in is so important. This is the only morally perfect God. He's a Person, with a will, not just a Force. And He's not any one of the thousand little squabbling, selfish bastards of mythology. And He doesn't have a dark side, He's not 'beyond good and evil'. He's *good*. And He's not a cosmic hypocrite: He practices what He preaches. And that's love."

"Okay, so I'm on board with half the world. But do Jews and Christians and Muslims all worship the same God? Muslims worship Allah."

"*Allah* is simply the Arabic word for God. You don't change Gods when you change languages."

"But Muslims say Muhammad is the greatest prophet, the perfect prophet, the infallible prophet, not Moses."

"So somebody's wrong there, either Jews or Muslims. But they're wrong about prophets, not about God. To say Muslims worship a different God because they believe a different prophet is like saying that if two Red Sox fans are arguing about whether Ted Williams or Carl Yastrzemski was the greatest hitter of all time, then they can't both be Red Sox fans."

"But Christians worship Jesus, and Jews and Muslims don't."

"And therefore ... what?"

"Therefore they're not worshipping the same God."

"Bad logic. That's like saying Protestants and Catholics don't worship the same Jesus because Catholics believe He's really present in the Eucharist and Protestants don't. The differences are terribly important, of course, but it doesn't mean they worship different Gods. There's only one, you know, and the rest of the world learned of Him through the same source: the Jews."

"But each religion has a different way to Heaven, a different way to be saved."

"To a certain extent, yes, although not *completely* different. And that's another terribly important question: 'What must I do to be saved?' But it's a different question than the question 'Who is God?'"

"But somebody's on the wrong road to Heaven, either Jews or Christians or Muslims."

"That doesn't logically follow. That's like saying that if you don't know whether it's Moses, Jesus, or Muhammad driving your car, then you're not really riding to your Father's house but to somebody else's house."

"Okay, so it's the same God in all three religions. I'm not really that interested in those theological questions. The only God I'm interested in is the God of love."

"And that's why we're here. *That's* the God of the Jews."

"Maybe it is, but I don't think that's the God of the Muslims. Is Allah the God of love?"

"According to the Koran, He is. 'Allah the compassionate, the merciful'—that's almost His middle name."

"But the Muslims keep fighting wars in His name. And so do Christians. And even when they're not fighting wars, and crusades, and burning heretics, they're still fighting wars with words—all three of them are—turning their religions into legalisms and theological arguments *and forgetting love.* They preach it, but they don't practice it. And that's a damn strong argument against religion, I think. Because actions speak louder than words."

"I agree with you, girl! All three groups have betrayed this revelation. But the revelation remains, and condemns their betrayal of it. If it didn't remain, if it wasn't there, if it wasn't valid, if it wasn't from God and we didn't have to take it seriously—why, then we wouldn't be shamed by it, and we wouldn't feel so guilty before God about all those wars, and we wouldn't be able to argue as you just did. Religion gives you the right to argue against religion!"

"That's a point, Mother. I've got to thank religion for that, at least."

"And remember, all three religions have produced the biggest saints in the world as well as the biggest sinners; the biggest lovers as well as the biggest haters."

"But the God of the Bible is always yelling at us."

"Why did your mama yell at you when you were little?"

"Because I acted up."

"Welcome to the human race. And did your mama forgive you and hug you and say she loved you even though you acted up?"

"Yeah."

"Where do you think she learned to do that? That's what God does."

"Oh."

"That's why He yells so much and thunders His threats and judgments in the Bible. He's like Mama. He gets upset by our betrayals of *love*. And He gets upset so much only because He loves us so much. Why did your mama get so upset about you when you were nasty? Because she loved you. You were *hers*. You weren't a stranger. Did your mama get upset about the ants in your yard eating each other and fighting with each other?"

"Ants? Why do you talk about ants?"

"Because compared to God we're smaller than ants. We can't hurt Him. Why doesn't He just ignore us when we fight and hate each other? Why would He take our sins so seriously if He didn't love us little ants so much?"

"I guess I see the point. He hates the sin so much only because He loves the sinner so much."

"Right! Why would He hate Libby's sins even more than your mama does if He didn't love Libby even more than your mama does?"

"Jesus didn't call Him 'Mama'."

"But He called Him 'Daddy'."

"'Father'."

"When He talked *about* Him, yes, He said, 'Father', but when He talked *to* Him He called Him 'Abba'. It means 'Daddy'. That's just as intimate as 'Mommy'."

"Why didn't He call Him 'Mommy' too?"

"I don't know. And I can't argue about what I don't know. I just know He invented both mommies and daddies, and that the Bible says He created us 'in His own image: male *and female*'. So whatever that is, it's not male chauvinism. But we don't have to solve that problem today. Let's start with what we know, not with what we don't know. And one of the things we know about Jesus' God is that He was the same God as the God of the Jews, isn't that right?"

"But wasn't His God the God of everybody?"

"The Creator of everybody, of course, and the lover of everybody, of course, but not everybody believed the same things about Him. Jesus believed what the Jews believed about Him, not what the Gentiles believed about Him. He believed the Jewish revelation, the Jewish Bible, the Jewish prophets."

"How do you know that?"

"Was Jesus a Jew? Or was He a Hindu? Or a Greek? Or was He an atheist, maybe?"

"Oh. Gotcha! But—but Christians believe He's *God*, the Son of God, and the Word of God, God-become-man. And Jews and Muslims don't believe that."

"That's right."

"Christians have this equation—Jesus equals God—and Jews and Muslims don't believe that equation. So there's nothing in common there."

"Yes there is. The second part of the equation is the same. It's the same God."

"But Christians believe this God became a man, and Jews and Muslims don't. So there's nothing common in *that* idea, the idea of God becoming a man."

"Yes there is. Tell me, why did this God become a man, according to Christianity?"

"To save us. To die for us."

"And why did God do that for us?"

"Out of love."

"And Jews believe He sent His words to us through Moses out of love. And Muslims believe that He sent His words to us through Muhammad out of love. Only words, not flesh, in those two religions, but—don't you see the parallel, at least? All three reveal the God of love. All three reveal the love of God. In all three religions, God bothers to speak to His little ants, who can't possibly hurt Him. Why? Out of love. Now that's a real revelation. That's not something we could have figured out. Why should God do that? It's like worrying about ants. That's just crazy! Like love. You don't have that in any other religion. Just these three. You have the moral command to love in all religions, but love doesn't go all the way up into God, and God doesn't love us, except in these three."

"That is impressive. But they still contradict each other, even if they are three words from the same God. And God can't contradict Himself. So two of them, at least, have to be wrong. Which two?"

"It's not that simple. Jesus connects and unites two of them, at least. Remember, Jesus was a Jew. (How easy it is to forget that!) His God was the God of the Jews, not a different God. He never told the Jews their Bible was wrong. He never told them to convert and start another religion. He said He was their Messiah, the One their religion promised, the One their prophets foretold. He said if they really believed Moses and the prophets, they would believe Him. And He promised to reconcile them with God, to plug them back into their God, the God He called His Father."

"That's a pretty big promise!"

"It sure is."

"So how do we know if it's true?"

"You mean how can we know whether Jesus was what He said He was or not?"

"Yeah. I think that's another reason for concentrating on this one religion instead of giving equal time to all of them: because of me, because that's where I am in fact coming from. I've got a lot of Christianity in my system, even though I'm not sure whether I believe it all or not. I can't pretend to be a neutral observer, like a Martian. If I'm going to know myself and my path, I have to start where I am. And that has something to do with who Jesus is."

"Let's go into that tomorrow."

"I hope the beach won't be this crowded tomorrow. I like one-on-one conversations better than parties."

"And today has been a sort of big religious party, on the beach with all the world's religions. But tomorrow we'll look at just one. If that one doesn't pan out, we'll look at others. But one at a time. Like people."

"We may eventually have to look at the other ones too, then—unless He blows them all out of the water."

JESUS

Libby came to the beach early the next morning, and Mother, as regular as the sun itself, showed up exactly at the appointed hour (eleven). The sun was already high in the sky and bright as itself (i.e., beyond all comparison), exploding unimaginable quantities of its fire out into the nowhere of space and everywhere on earth. Libby wondered how it could keep doing that for billions of years. She glanced in its direction and quickly turned away before being blinded.

"Ready to continue climbing the ladder?" Mother asked.

"It's been a surprising script to me so far", Libby admitted. "I never thought the rungs on the ladder could be so clear and solid."

"Rungs on a ladder *have* to be clear and solid if we're going to get anywhere. Imagine trying to climb on mush."

"I don't have to imagine that; I've been doing it most of my life, I think."

"Well, we certainly climbed out of mush yesterday, because we climbed as far as the Jews, and they're definitely not mush. And if we look deeper at them, we have to look at the most famous Jew of all. Because that's where the story goes. That's what happens next."

"Jesus."

"Yes. That's where He shows up: among this strange little people who claim to be so different, and are."

"That always bothered me, by the way", Libby interrupted. "They claim to be 'God's chosen people'. That sounds so arrogant, so provincial."

"But it's just the opposite. It's the humblest possible interpretation of the data."

"What data?"

"The data of history. Their survival, despite all the odds. Their success. Their contributions to civilization, out of all proportion to their size. There's nothing and nobody in history like them. Did they do all that by themselves? If so, they must be superior. But they say it's not from them but from God. They give God all the credit. That's what 'the chosen people' means. Does that sound arrogant, or does that sound humble?"

"Maybe their God is their invention too."

"Then they're even more superior! That's the fundamental question about them: Is even their God *their* invention? Or are they God's invention?"

"That's a nice take on it. I never thought of it that way."

"You should have; it's in their Bible. You must have read that old book some time."

"Oh, yeah."

"Then you know how that God works. He doesn't choose the best or the smartest or the strongest to be His prophets, so *they* don't get any special glory. He chooses *schmucks, schlemiels.*"

"Losers."

"Yes. His winners are our losers. There's no profit in being a prophet."

"I guess that means the Gentiles are a non-prophet organization, and the Jews are a non-profit organization."

"Touché! And the Jews are simply His collective prophet to the whole world. Like all the prophets, they're not chosen for their own sake but for the sake of their mission to the world."

"And that mission is . . . ?"

"To tell the world who God is, and what He wants, and what He's doing."

"And Jesus completes that job?"

"Gotcha!"

"So He's the last prophet."

"More than a prophet. He *claims* to be much more than a prophet, and either He is or He isn't. If He is, well, then He is. And if He isn't, then He's much *less* than a prophet. He's a liar and a fake."

"Christians claim He's divine."

"Because *Jesus* claimed to be divine."

"How?"

"He called God His Father. A dog doesn't call a man his father; only a man can do that. He claimed to forgive sins—all sins, any sins. Only God can do that. He even spoke the unspeakable name, God's own private name, the name that no Jew ever even dares to pronounce because only God bears that name: in English it's 'I AM'. When 'Doubting Thomas' saw Him after He rose from the dead, and called Him 'My Lord and my God', He didn't correct him. And there's more . . . There are His miracles, and His Resurrection . . ."

"Okay. I know the story. So He *claimed* to be God, or the Son of God. That doesn't prove He *was*. He *believed* it, and Christians *believe* it, but how do you *prove* it? How do you go from faith to fact? There's a gap there."

"Yes there is."

"Especially with a claim like that. How is it *possible*? He's obviously a man; how can He be both God and man, Creator and creature, infinite and finite, eternal and temporal, immortal and mortal, all at the same time? It's a contradiction. It's not logically possible."

"Is it logically possible to write a story about yourself?"

"Of course. What's that got to do with it? That's totally different."

"No it's not. It's similar; it's an analogy. If I write a story about myself, I'm both the creator of the story and the creature I create in my story. Same person, one person, but with two natures, both the transcendent creator of the story and a character immanent in the story at the same time. Alfred Hitchcock always put himself into his own movies as a minor character, sometimes a pedestrian crossing a street. Do you mean to say that he can do that and God can't?"

"Oh. I guess I can't say that. God can do anything."

"Anything that has any meaning. I don't think He can make a square circle, because that doesn't mean anything, that's just nonsense syllables."

"Can He make a rock too big for Him to lift, then?"

"Nope. That's meaningless too: a rock too big for infinite power to lift—that's a self-contradictory concept."

"Okay, so God can become a man without ceasing to be God. That's logic."

"It's also love."

"You mean He did it out of love for us."

"Of course. But I also mean that love gave Him the *power* to do it. If God is love, then to say that God could not do that is to say that love cannot do that."

"Oh. That's true too, I guess. I never looked at it that way. Okay, so let's say Jesus is God."

"Wait. I think you're going too fast. 'Let's say'—that's too easy. Just saying it doesn't make it so. The claim has to be tested. The gap has to be crossed."

"How?"

"By looking at the alternative. What if He *isn't*, or *wasn't*, who He claimed to be? What if He was only a man and only *claimed* to be God? What would that make Him?"

"A liar."

"How big of a liar?"

"As big as any liar can ever be."

"So He's not only a liar but an imposter, a fake, a charlatan, a false prophet, who wants you to worship Him and give Him your life and your soul and trust Him with your eternal salvation. He can't really save your soul and take you to Heaven, but He says He can and He wants you to sign it over to Him. Who does that sound like?"

"The Devil. That's what the Devil does. Sign the contract. Give me your soul."

"So Jesus is either God or the Devil."

"Wow. That sounds pretty extreme."

"It is pretty extreme."

"That doesn't sound real. Reality usually has alternatives in between extremes."

"Not always. Has anybody ever been partly pregnant? Or neither alive nor dead?"

"That's different."

"Yes, it is. So let's look at something that's not different. Let's look at some other mere human being claiming what He claimed. Take me. Suppose I said I was God, and I alone could save you from your sins and get you to Heaven? Suppose I asked you to worship me as God? Now tell me, could I be just a good human being, just a wise moral teacher, if I said *that*?"

"No way. You're either the Big Lie or the Big Truth. Your claim is too big to be anything else."

"Exactly."

"But how can we be sure Jesus *wasn't* the Devil? Or at least inspired by the Devil?"

"That would make Him one of the wickedest men who ever lived, if He knew He was lying, or else one of the most insane men who ever lived if He didn't know it and really believed He was God—wouldn't it?"

"Yes."

"Does anybody in the whole world ever believe that about Jesus? That He was one of the wickedest men who ever lived? Or one of the most insane? Is that what Jews say? Muslims? Buddhists? Hindus? Do even atheists ever say that?"

"No. They all say He was a great moralist, a good man. That sounds more ... more likely, more possible."

"Not if we ask the question we just asked."

"What question?"

"The simplest of all questions: Is what He said true or false? Is He who He claimed to be, or not? If we dare to ask that simple question, then no matter how we answer it, then 'just a good man but not God' is the one and only thing He couldn't *possibly* be."

"So we have only two alternatives, and they're two extremes."

"Yep."

"That still doesn't prove He's the good extreme instead of the bad one."

"It does if we look at Him. What did He teach? In one word, how did He tell us to live?"

"Love. Live in love."

"And did He practice what He preached? Did He love people, and help them, and cure them, and teach them? Did He sacrifice His life for them? Did He give

His Blood for them? Or did He take their blood, like Dracula?"

"The answer to that one looks pretty clear."

"Like the sun."

"Why doesn't everybody see that, then?"

"Maybe it's *too* clear, too bright, too extreme—like the sun."

"But it looks so simple, the way you put it: just look at the human face of Jesus. You don't need faith, you don't need to believe He's God, you just need to get to know Him as you'd get to know Socrates or Saint Francis—and then it's as plain as the sun that He's not the wickedest man in the world. But it just can't be that simple."

"Why not? Maybe that's why He came down from Heaven: to make it that simple and obvious to us."

"But that's—that's more like science than like philosophy. It's data, not pure theory. You didn't give me abstract definitions and explanations and creeds about the Trinity, and you didn't give me ideologies and theologies and theories—you just gave me *data*. Concrete data. Evidence. That's like science. You go into the lab, and you look at the evidence. You don't just *think* it, you *see* it."

"That's exactly what He said; 'Come and see.' "

"But He said that to people back then. It's a little too late in the day for me. Two thousand years too late."

"Not at all. You can still meet Him."

"Where? In my own feelings? Is this rung going to turn into mush now?"

"No. Meet Him in the Gospels, and meet His saints in the world."

Libby was silent. "So it's still 'Come and see.' Why doesn't everybody see, then?"

"Because they don't come. You can't see if you don't come, if you don't look."

"Wait a minute. That has to be too simple. What about all the other data? We can't ignore any data at all if we're open-minded."

"Fine. Let's look at the other data. Let's look at everything. What 'other data' do you have in mind?"

"Oh, Bible-bashing Fundamentalists, and the Spanish Inquisition, and the sack of Constantinople, and pogroms against Jews, and 'good Christian' men who beat their women, and hypocritical priests who bugger little boys. How's that for starters?"

"That's evidence about Christians, about some of the people who claim to be His followers. They include some horrible sinners. How is that evidence about *Him*? Did He either preach or practice anything like that?"

"No, but they did all that crap in His name."

"Yes—and that awful irony is exactly my point. Why is that so horrible to do that in His name? Why is that more horrible than just doing it? Only because His name is holy. Only because He's perfect. If He was a devil like them, then they wouldn't be hypocritical at all to do all that evil in His name."

"Yeah, I see that. But if He's the only perfect one, He's alone up there in the sun, and we're all still stuck in the dark."

"But we're not. We have the light."

"But we don't act like it."

"Some do. What about the saints? I've explained the sinners, how do you explain the saints if Jesus isn't the saint maker, as they all say He is? Where did all those saints come from? Who makes Mother Teresa tick? That's data too. Saints are data just as much as sinners are."

"Okay. So there are lovers and haters, and the lovers do what He taught and the haters don't. What does that prove?"

"Let's look. Let's look at where they come from. Where did the hate come from? The haters' hate came from themselves. They're selfish. But the lovers' love—where did that come from? How can *un*selfishness come from the self? It comes from Above."

"How do you know it all comes from Above? Who knows where it comes from? Psychology is full of mysteries."

"*They* know where it comes from. The saints all say the same thing: that it comes from Him, as all this sunlight comes from the sun."

"So they say that. That doesn't mean it's true."

"Are they all fools? Are saints all stupid? Can you believe that?—that the better they are, the holier they are, the more unselfish and loving they are, the more wrong they are about where that love comes from, and the more wrong they are about Him? Can you believe that the more right their religious practice is, the more wrong their religious belief is, even though they all say that their practice came *from* their belief? Can you believe that?"

"Why not? I don't want to, but tell me why."

"Because it's terrible psychology. The human heart would have to be split into opposite halves then. The half that led to love and goodness would contradict the half that led to truth. So you could never go in both directions at once. The more saintly and unselfish and loving you are, the more superstitious and wrong and deluded you would be—about that very love. That's a terrible psychology! Can you believe *that*?"

"No, I can't believe that terrible psychology. But there aren't many saints in my world, Mother. Some pretty good people, sure, but not saints. I never met Saint Francis or Mother Teresa. My world is full of mean streets and mean people. There's not much data there about saints."

"Then I suggest you expand your world. Because I know it's a lot bigger than that."

"I guess we just have to agree to disagree there, Mother. Unless you can tell me what street to go to, to find saints."

"I can. Ever hear of Roxbury?"

"Of course. When I was a social worker, a lot of my cases lived there. That's what I mean: mean streets, broken lives, broken people, broken families."

"Let me give you the address in Roxbury where you can meet Mother Teresa."

"You're kidding."

"No, not at all. Her Missionaries of Charity are in Roxbury right now, picking up the pieces of those broken lives and loving those broken people. Visit them. Meet them. Talk to them. They are saints. They are like Mother Teresa. They have her joy amid all the brokenness. They are the happiest people you will ever meet."

"You're not kidding, are you?"

"No, I am not. I think I know you, Libby. You're skeptical, tough-minded, open-minded, and scientific. You want concrete data. Good. You can find it. You can find it there. Just go there, and meet them, and if you have any doubts about Jesus, they will cure your doubts better than any argument in the world. You will never forget them, even if you try."

Libby was surprised and silent. Mother added, "And you may *want* to try, because you will be haunted by them, as people were haunted by Jesus."

"I never thought the argument would move in that direction!"

"Why not? It's His direction. 'Come and see', remember?"

Libby was silent.

"So? Do you want their address, or what?"

Libby was still silent.

"Are you afraid to *look*?"

"I'm asking myself the same question."

"And are you getting any answers?"

"I'm not afraid to look, but maybe I'm afraid to *see*. Because maybe I'll look into the sun and hurt my eyes. Maybe it's the sun that I'm afraid of."

"The 'sun' of God, you mean?"

"Yeah."

"But we just agreed that He was love. Are you afraid of *love*?"

Libby smiled a little rueful, ironic smile. "Maybe I am. Love isn't a nice pat on the head, you know. It's more like an earthquake."

"You are a wise woman, Libby. You will go places in your life."

"I've already gone to too many places in my life so far."

"But love wasn't one of them, was it? The kind of love He is, I mean."

"No, but I got a feeling maybe love is going to be one of those places. I promise you I will visit these women when I get back to the mainland. But first we have to finish our conversations, don't we? Let's assume Jesus is in place now on our ladder. Where do we go next?"

"We go to the beach again tomorrow. One rung at a time, remember?"

Dialogue Nine

CATHOLICS

The next day was rainy, and Mother suggested, by phone, that Libby come to the House for conversation and bread when the rain let up that afternoon. Libby happily accepted.

"Let me guess what we're going to talk about today", Libby said, right off. "If I believe in Jesus, that makes me a Christian, right? (I sort of always thought I was, but I didn't know it for sure.) So the next question has to be: What kind of a Christian should I be? Which church should I join?"

"That's the logic of the ladder, all right", replied Mother.

"But I don't really want to get into that. I don't trust churches. I'm also bored by them. And I'm frankly suspicious of missionaries. They're salesmen. Whatever product they want you to buy, it's always their company's. But there are a lot of other companies out there."

"So you'd rather just smile equally at all the salesmen instead of choosing to buy anything from any one of them?"

"That's pretty much me, yes."

"So you don't want to enter one of the houses, but just stay outside in the street, looking at them all but not living in any one?"

"Houses are boxes. I don't want to be confined. I'd rather be out on the beach. I guess it's spiritual claustrophobia. I also don't like to be forced to choose."

"But if you have a house, you have the choice to go inside or outside. And if you don't have a house, you don't have a choice: you're homeless, you have to live outside in the street. And as far as choices are concerned, you've made eight choices already."

"True. I did, and that's not my nature. I don't like to narrow my options. I like the street better than the houses, I guess. And I'm especially reluctant to climb whatever rung you're going to hold out before me today, because I see that as limiting my options too much. I don't know what house you're selling me, but I don't want to buy a house, maybe not ever and certainly not today. And I don't want to prejudice my house-hunting by looking only at the one you're selling, whichever one it is. Nothing personal, Mother; it's not you, it's me. That's just the way I am. By the way, what are you, anyway? Let's have full disclosure here, please."

"Well, you might call me a little bit of everything", Mother replied. "I come from a Jewish background. I'm a Jewish Christian, or a Messianic Jew. But I'm also a Catholic, a Roman Catholic. And I love the Eastern Orthodox liturgies, so I attend an Eastern-Rite Church most of the time. But most of my friends are Protestants, and I love and respect them deeply and learn a lot from all of them: everyone from Quakers to High-Church Anglicans, with a lot of Evangelicals in between."

"So you live in one house but you love all the houses on your block."

"Exactly."

"That's quite a variety."

"So are the people who live here", Mother replied. "Whatever you find here, it won't be narrowness. No two are alike. We have almost everybody you could imagine here, except Muslims—so far, anyway."

Libby verified this when she met the other "Housebugs", as they called themselves, that evening, over supper (which she helped Mother cook and found incredibly cheap, fresh, and delicious). There was Lazarus, whom Mother described as "the oldest Jew I ever met". There was Eva, a sweet, sensitive nature-mystic, who had been a thalidomide baby and had no arms and no hair. There was Evan, an argumentative but humble Dutch Calvinist seminarian. There was Mister Mumm, a seraphically bland, quiet, pious man. When Libby asked about his religious affiliation, Mother replied, "Oh, he's a kind of Universalist. He's just an angel." And there were Diddly and Squat. One was an Evangelical Anglican from Uganda and the other a Caribbean who seemed to Libby to mix something like Pentecostalism with something like voodoo, although she could easily be wrong about both sides of that mix. She found it very strange that she could never remember which of these two men wore which of these two religious clothes, even though the two men were the most comically different people in the house and their clothing styles were as different as a tuxedo and a T-shirt. Finally, there was Gus, their smiling "village atheist", as he called himself, the only nonpermanent resident of the House, who was about to leave for a job teaching theology at a Jesuit university. They all came home from work at suppertime, so Mother and Libby were alone all afternoon for conversation over cooking and cleaning in the enormous kitchen.

Mother began, "I suspect you don't want to talk about churches, but I think you have to."

"Why?"

"Because if you decide to be a Christian you have to decide which kind of Christian to be."

"But there are thousands of different kinds. There are thousands of options."

"Yes, but there are only two basic options: Catholic and Protestant."

"What about Eastern Orthodox?"

"Oh, they're 99% Catholic, except for the stuff about the Pope."

"And Anglicans?"

"The High-Church ones are Protestants who think they're Catholics."

"That's funny, but is it fair?"

"No, I'm half-kidding. It's not that simple, really. And I'm not that stupid."

"And I'm not that stupid either. I know there are a lot of differences between Protestants and Catholics: about the Pope and about sacraments and about church authority and about saints and about Mary and about Purgatory and about the Mass and about interpreting the Bible and about the Reformation—how can anyone but a theologian see their way through all that stuff to make an intelligent choice? I think most people just find themselves in whatever church their parents found themselves in. But that's not for me. I've always been the rebel. If they do it one way, I've got to do it the other way."

"But 'they' aren't here now, are they?" Mother asked.

"No. But I am. So here I am in the religious cafeteria, and I don't know what food to choose. I don't even know *how* to choose. Or why. Why do I have to pick just one and leave all the others? I like some things about Protestants—they don't have to kowtow to a pope, and they come in so many different denominations. But I like some things about Catholics too—they've got the art and the history and the philosophy and the style and the saints, and more smells and bells. But I know I can't decide by counting kowtows or by counting smells and bells. The Protestant churches look like a lot of little new cars, and the Catholic Church looks like one big old car, but I like both: I like little cars and big cars too. Even if I do have to choose, I don't know how. I wish there was a simple, easy way."

"There is", Mother replied.

"How?"

"Remember what we said yesterday, and then apply it today. How did you decide about Christianity yesterday? By deciding about Christ, right? Not by looking at all the Christian creeds, or all the things in the Christian Bible, or all the many different things Christ taught, with the eye of a theologian, or a philosopher, and then figuring it all out and deciding to accept them, one by one. You did it by accepting a Person, a concrete, historical Person and what He claimed for Himself: that He is divine. If He's divine, then everything He says must be true, whatever the details. Isn't that how we thought our way into it yesterday?"

"Yes. But that's because there's only one Christ. But there are thousands of Christianities, thousands of churches."

"So let's look at just how Christ made it easy for you to decide about Him, and then let's see if there's any parallel way to decide about churches. If we can find a general principle here, we can apply it to different questions."

"Fine, if we can do that."

"He made it easy for you to decide to believe in Him because He didn't want only brilliant philosophers and theologians and scholars to come to believe in Him. He wants everybody, because He wants to save everybody. Not everybody can decide what theology is true, but everybody can meet this Person and decide whether this Person is true."

"So He made it easy by making it concrete instead of abstract."

"Exactly. It's a kind of Principle of Concreteness. He didn't say, 'I teach the truth, and these fifty things are the truth.' He said, 'I AM the Truth, the Logos, the Mind of God; I'm the Son of God, and I'm the *one and only* Son of God.' So there's one and only one question you have to ask to decide whether to become a Christian: Is Jesus the Divine Person He claims to be or not?"

"Right. But how can we apply that to churches?"

"The way He did. *He* gave us a Church, one Church. He didn't wait for us to invent one, or more than one. He made it concrete and historical and visible. Just look at the New Testament."

"The whole thing?"

"Yes, the whole thing."

"That will take a while."

"Not if you have a concordance that lists all the verses where a word is used. Just take a concordance and look up every verse in the New Testament that uses the word *church*. If you do that, you'll get a pretty good picture of the Church He gave us. And if you also read the early Christian writers, the 'Church Fathers', you'll get an even clearer, stronger picture of what the first Christians believed about the Church."

"And if I do that, what will I find?"

"The Nicene Creed summarizes it in four words, the four 'marks of the Church'. It says, 'I believe in one, holy, catholic, and apostolic Church.' The Church is *one*, not many. And it's *holy*, which means 'set apart' from everything else. And it's *catholic*, which means 'universal', one Church for all nations and races and all kinds of people. And it's *apostolic*: it's the Church founded by Jesus' twelve Apostles and those they authorized as their successors—which is simply a historical fact. That's what's meant by 'apostolic succession'. And it goes back to the beginning of the Church: the New Testament calls the Apostles' successors, 'presbyters' or 'bishops'."

"So that's the *Catholic* Church, then."

"That's the only one that has all four of those 'marks of the Church', especially 'apostolic succession'. You see, the issue of 'Which church?' is surprisingly simple, because Jesus made it simple. It's simply a historical fact that He founded one visible Church and commissioned His Apostles to keep it going by authorizing successors. And He authorized them to teach *in His name*. He said, 'He who hears you hears me" (Luke 10:16). And it's also simply a historical fact that the Apostles did authorize successors, 'bishops', and that that line of 'apostolic succession' continued for two thousand years as a single, continuous, visible institution."

"What about all the Protestant churches?"

"They're all five hundred years old or less. The Catholic Church is two thousand years old."

"It's that simple? It can't be that simple."

"He made it that simple."

"What do Protestants say to that? They must have some answer to that."

"They claim that *they* go back to the early Church, and that the Catholic Church doesn't. They say the Catholic Church is the new kid on the block, not them.

They say the Catholic Church is like a ship whose hull is full of barnacles—foreign organisms that didn't come on the original Noah's Ark—and that all that the Protestant Reformers did was to scrape off those barnacles and restore the Ark to what it was like when Jesus constructed it."

"Oh. So that's how they answer the Catholic argument that it was only Luther and Calvin who founded their churches five hundred years ago while Jesus founded the Catholic Church two thousand years ago."

"Yes."

"I can see that. They'd have to say that. There's no other answer they could have."

"So you see it *is* one simple question, really."

"Yes. But that doesn't mean there's one simple answer to it, or one simple way to find the answer."

"But there is. There's a simple way to test who's right there."

"You mean logic? Are you going to argue that Catholic theology is clearly right and Protestant theology is clearly wrong if we think clearly and logically about each of those issues that separate them? If that's where you're going next, I think I can save us both some time, because I don't have a lifetime and a half to explore theology, thank you very much. There are too many differences, and they're too abstract and difficult, and it would take forever to explore them all, and even then, I don't think I could be sure."

"You're right. No, there's another way, and it's concrete, not abstract, and it asks just one question, not many, and it doesn't take a lifetime, and you can be sure of it. Remember our Principle of Concreteness."

"What is that other way, then, the concrete way?"

"Just look at the facts instead of the theories. Look at history. Look at the early Church. Look at the early Christian writers and see if they're Protestant or Catholic. All that Catholic stuff that Protestants don't believe because they don't see it clearly in the Bible—the Mass and the Real Presence and the authority of the Bishop of Rome, the Pope, and prayers to saints and the sacraments—is all that stuff barnacles on the Ark, or animals in it? Does it come from inside or outside? Are they original passengers or parasites?"

"That makes sense. But there are a lot of 'barnacles' to look at. Which one do you think is the most important one?"

"It has to be something about Jesus Himself."

"Right. But both Catholics and Protestants believe in Jesus, and everything He said in the Bible. They just interpret His words differently."

"That's true."

"So we're back in abstract theology, arguing about which interpretation is right. Because today there are a thousand different churches with a thousand different interpretations. And we'll probably get stuck on that road."

"Actually, it's more like twenty-five thousand different denominations. No, there's another way. Maybe I can explain it by a silly-sounding thought experiment. Just imagine that when you looked at these thousands of churches you found one church teaching that Jesus was still here and that He looked like a gray squirrel. The people in this church believed everything about Jesus in the Bible, but they also believed that that same Jesus was this gray squirrel, and they worshipped that gray squirrel as God. What would you say about them?"

"That they were crazy, of course, if I know any psychology at all. And if I know any theology at all, I'd say they were worshipping an idol. That's the First Commandment, isn't it?—not to worship idols."

"Exactly. That would be a more terrible mistake than anything else about Jesus, wouldn't it? More terrible than getting some doctrine wrong, like whether He predestined you, or just *how* His death saved you, or how the three Persons of the Trinity were related?"

"Yes, of course."

"But what if these 'gray-squirrel Christians' were right?"

"Okay, that's a bit hard to imagine. . . . But if they were, I suppose, then, that everybody else would be wrong—wrong *about Christ*—because they wouldn't have Christ in the gray squirrel, and the gray-squirrel Christians would."

"They might still have the whole Christ in their hearts and souls, but not in their world. They might still have Him subjectively but not objectively, if He *was* really there in the gray squirrel, but they didn't believe that."

"Are you saying that Catholics are like 'gray-squirrel Christians' because they believe Jesus is in the Church?"

"In the Mass. In the Eucharist. In that thing that looks like a little wafer of bread. Catholics worship that. They adore that as God. They believe it only *looks* like bread, but it's really Jesus. That's how they interpret His words 'This is My Body'. They interpret it literally. Most Protestants don't. They interpret it as 'This is a holy *symbol of* My Body'."

"Oh, well, then, if that's the way it is, then I guess the next question is which kind of Protestant I should be, now that we've gotten that 'gray-squirrel' craziness out of the way."

"Wait a minute! I thought you agreed that we should decide what to believe not by abstract theologizing and philosophizing but by looking at the concrete facts of history."

"Yeah, I said that. So what?"

"You're going back on that now. You're not looking at what the early Christians actually did believe and teach. You're looking at the issue abstractly, abstracted from history, as an *idea*, and you're judging the idea to be so obviously illogical that you have to reject it."

"I guess I am. But that seems reasonable."

"It also seemed reasonable to say that Jesus was only a good man and not God, didn't it? Until we looked at history and found out that He *claimed* to be God, and then we had to confront that claim. Isn't that right?"

"Yes . . ."

"So now if we find that the early Church *claimed* that Jesus was really, truly, literally, objectively present in what looked like that wafer of bread—if we found out that all the Christians in the world believed that and taught that and claimed that they got it from Jesus Himself and His Apostles—if they all taught that for the first fifteen hundred years—well, then, that would change things, wouldn't it?"

"Oh, I see. Good grief. Fifteen hundred years of 'gray-squirrel Christians'? And are you saying that that's what we do find when we look at history?"

"Yes. That's what we find when we look for historical facts instead of arguing about theories."

"But when we look at the theory, the idea, the belief, the claim—it just looks so . . . so crazy."

"Like believing this man who was born a little baby was Almighty God?"

"Oh. Yeah, a lot like that."

"So now since we have clear historical data, even though maybe we don't have clear theological data, let's compare the two historical claims, not the theological claims. Let's compare the historical claim of the Protestants, the 'barnacle Christians' with the claim of the Catholics, the 'gray-squirrel Christians'. The 'barnacle' theory may seem to make more sense, until you look at the historical facts. And we have to test theories by facts, don't we?"

"How can you call any theological belief a 'fact'?"

"I don't mean the beliefs themselves as ideas, I mean the facts of history. Which theological belief is true may not be a 'fact', but which people believed it—that *is* a fact, and a historical fact. So let's look at the historical facts and find out whether the Protestant theory or the Catholic theory about Church history fits the historical facts. So the question is simple: Did the early Church believe the 'gray-squirrel' theory or not?"

"And the answer—is that as simple as the question?"

"If you look, you will see. There was not a single Christian in the world who *didn't* believe in the 'Real Presence' of Christ in the Eucharist for the first thousand years. Then there was one guy, Berenger of Tours, who denied it—I think it was around the eleventh century— and the Church labeled him a heretic for not believing what all Christians had always believed. So here are three historical facts: Christians believed that for fifteen hundred years, and Catholics still do, and most Protestants don't, or believe only a weaker version of it."

"Oh. But what about all those *other* Catholic beliefs that aren't in the Bible that Protestants don't believe? Are they barnacles?"

"If you look at the Christian writings before the Reformation, you won't find a single one of those doctrines that's controversial, that's argued about and rejected. In other words, there were no Protestants in the early Church. There's a continuity, not a break. The Church didn't become Catholic instead of Protestant in A.D. 313, or 500, or 800, or 1200."

"Okay, that may be true about the Church, but what about the relation between the Church and the Bible? Protestants believe only the Bible as the infallible word of God, not the teachings of the Church, right? What did the early Christians believe on that issue?"

"Well, let's look. Take Saint Augustine. He's the most influential Christian writer of all time, outside the Bible. Let's see what he said about the Bible and the Church. This is what he said: 'I would not believe the Bible if it were not for the authority of the Church.' "

"Oh. What about earlier writers?"

"They all appealed to the Bishop of Rome as the final authority to settle disputes. The Bishops of Rome were successors of Saint Peter, who was the first Bishop of Rome. Later, they used the word *pope* for that position. And those are all historical facts too, not theories."

"So if the Protestants are right, Augustine is one of the barnacles."

"At least when he taught that you need the authority of the Church to certify the authority of the Bible, yes."

"And nobody scraped off those Catholic 'barnacles' for fifteen hundred years."

"No."

"So Saint Francis of Assisi and Thomas Aquinas and Bernard of Clairvaux—they were all full of barnacles."

"Yes."

"Why would God allow that?"

"Well, Protestants believe He didn't. He raised up prophets like Luther and Calvin to reform it."

"But not for fifteen hundred years. Did God fall asleep for fifteen hundred years and woke up only when Luther and Calvin were born?"

"Good question."

"And when these Protestant prophets started contradicting what the Church had always taught, how did God expect everyone to know that He was speaking through *them* and not through the Pope and the bishops and everyone else in the Church? How did God expect us to know that Luther and Calvin were His authorities, not Augustine and Aquinas and the popes and the Church councils and the whole rest of the Church that had been teaching things like the Real Presence for fifteen hundred years?"

"Good question, girl. Don't ask me, ask them."

"And when did this ridiculous 'gray-squirrel' idolatry begin, if it isn't true? When did people start believing in 'gray-squirrel Christianity'? When did they start worshipping wine and bowing to bread, thinking it was God? When did this begin?"

"Ask the books. Ask the data. I think you will find the answer pretty clearly, especially if you read the sixth chapter of John's Gospel. It began with Jesus."

"And why didn't anybody protest this ridiculous-sounding idea? Where were the protests of the Protestants for the first fifteen hundred years? Where were the controversies, where were the arguments? Where were the Reformers before the Reformation?"

"Actually, the first protesters go back to Jesus' time too, but they weren't Protestants. They weren't Christians at all. They didn't become Christians *because becoming a Christian meant believing that.* You can find that original protest in the same place as you find the original teaching: John 6."

"So the people who didn't believe Jesus' claims—they got Jesus crucified for it, right?"

"Right. Which is exactly what they should have done, if they were right. A mere man who claims to be God, and claims to turn bread into Himself, doesn't deserve to be worshipped, or even admired and followed as a good person. He's a blasphemer and an idolater, or else He's insane. He deserves either to be executed for blasphemy or at least put into an insane asylum. And they didn't have insane asylums in those days, just as we don't have executions for blasphemy these days."

"And here's another question: If the fallible Church got it wrong about the Real Presence in the Eucharist and all those other Catholic doctrines, why couldn't the fallible Church have gotten it wrong about Jesus? And about the Trinity—in the Church's early creeds that the Protestants *do* accept."

"Another good question!"

"How do Protestants answer it?"

"They say it isn't clear in the Bible what the Eucharist is but it *is* clear just from the Bible who Jesus is and what the Trinity is."

"But it isn't!"

"No, it isn't. The early creeds defined His divinity, and said He was one Person with two natures, and the creeds defined the Trinity—because those clear definitions aren't in the Bible either. All the heretics appealed to the Bible, but the Bible wasn't enough. The Bible didn't interpret itself. That's why they needed Church councils and creeds."

"But Protestants accept those creeds, don't they?—the ones that define the nature of Christ and the Trinity?"

"Yes."

"But not the later ones, that define the Catholic doctrines that they reject."

"Right."

"Why? How can Protestants accept the early creeds but not the later ones if they both come from the same authority, the Church?"

"They think the later ones contradict the Bible, and the earlier ones don't."

"Well, what's wrong with that answer?"

"What's wrong with it is that that's exactly what all the early heretics thought. They all appealed to the Bible. They believed that those doctrines about Christ and the Trinity that the Church councils defined contradicted the Bible and their alternatives didn't. But the Church said to them, 'No, you're wrong. It's you who contradict the Bible, not us.' And all that is simply historical fact too, not theological theory."

"And why do the Protestants accept the Bible if they don't trust the Church that gave it to them? How can a fallible Church write an infallible Book?"

"Another good question! A very fundamental question."

"Here's an even more fundamental question: Why do they trust Jesus? How do they know He's God? Can't you interpret the Bible so that He isn't? Didn't some heretics do that?"

"A lot of people still do."

"So this is not just about the Bible. It's about Jesus. To get Him right, you need the Church."

"Yes. And that too is a historical fact, not a theory."

"Wait. Don't some Catholics deny Jesus is God, just as some Protestants do?"

"Yes, but they're contradicted by their Church, like a storm stopped by a sea wall. The Protestants don't have that sea wall. Their churches get flooded by the new ideas that Catholics call heresies. They change. They give up some of their old teachings, because they don't think they're infallible. The Catholic Church doesn't do that."

"But there are still Catholic unbelievers in the Catholic Church. Some of their theologians are heretics."

"Sure. But those Catholic unbelievers are bad Catholics, while the Protestant unbelievers are only bad Calvinists by being good Baptists, or bad Baptists by being good Calvinists."

"Oh. So—bottom line—there are two big reasons for believing the Church: to be sure to get the Bible right and to be sure to get Jesus right."

"You see it, girl."

"Is it really that simple? Am I really that logical? How did I do that? I'm not a philosopher."

"I think you got the logic right because you got the history right. I think you see the theory because you see the facts."

"It feels a lot like the argument about Jesus yesterday. It really is simpler than it looks."

"Yes. There's a close parallel between the two arguments, about Jesus and about the Church. Our argument about Jesus started with the fact of His claim: He claimed more for Himself than any other man in history—any sane man, anyway. He claimed to be God. And the argument said that either He is or He isn't. And if He is, you worship Him, and if He isn't, you crucify Him, or put Him in an insane asylum. And here's the parallel: the Catholic

Church also claims more for herself than any other church—
any sane one, anyway. She claims to be infallible, and the
only Church, and the one established by Jesus Himself. If
that's not true, if no church can be infallible, then that
Catholic claim is a terribly arrogant claim, a claim to be
the very voice of God. That's blasphemous. Only prophets claim more than human wisdom—both false prophets
and true prophets. So either the Catholic Church is a false
prophet or a true prophet. And if she's a false prophet,
that's terrible. That's a merely human voice claiming to
be a divine voice. That's almost like a mere man claiming
to be God. So the same argument about Jesus holds for
the Church."

"But it's not easy to believe any one of those three
things: either that that Church is infallible or that that
wafer is Jesus or that that man is God."

"That's true. You still have two options: Yes or No."

"And that's a very big claim, and whether it's true or
not is a very big question, and there's a very big gap
between the two answers. How can you decide that big
a question?"

"The same way a first-century Jew could decide about
Jesus: meet Him."

"You mean meet the argument?"

"I didn't say, 'Meet the argument'; I said, 'Meet Him.'
He didn't say, 'Meet my arguments.' He invited us to
meet Him. He said, 'Come and see.' Use facts instead of
theories. Get it straight from the horse's mouth. That's
how we've come as far as we have today, and that's how
we can go the next step."

"That's fine for a first-century Jew, but how can we
meet Him *today*? How can a Christian today decide
whether or not to be a Catholic? And how is that the

same way a first-century Jew could decide whether or not to be a Christian?"

"Come and see. Ask Him. You can still do that if He's still here."

"'Ask Him'? What do you mean?"

"Go to Mass. If you already believe in Christ but not in the Church, ask Christ whether that's Him there, behind the appearances of bread in that little white round thing that all those people are worshipping and believing in. Ask Him: Does He love the fact that all those people worship Him there, or does He hate this ridiculous idolatry? Go into a Catholic church, put yourself in front of that little gold box that Catholics call the tabernacle, where they believe Jesus is really present, and ask Jesus Himself whether He wants you to run forward or backward. Does He want you to run up to the Host in a flame of faith and love, or does He want to you run back away from this pagan idol worship as fast as you can go? Just ask Him. Literally."

"Are you saying you know what will happen if I do?"

"I'm saying only what He said: 'Seek, and you will find.'"

"But if I don't *know* whether He's really there, how can I pray to Him as if He *is* really there?"

"The same way the open-minded agnostic can pray, 'God, if you are really there, please let me know.' Just say: 'Jesus, if you are really there, then please, please draw me there, where You really are. And if You are *not* there, then please, please don't let me be drawn to where You are not.' And then stop worrying and trust Him that He will do what He promised. If you do the seeking, He'll take care of the finding."

"Mother, it's amazing how you make the most complex thing in the world the most simple thing in the world. How do you get it to be so simple?"

"By looking at the center of the circle instead of the circumference. By looking at Him."

"I admire that in you, Mother; but I can't believe something just because you believe it."

"Of course not. But it's not a matter between you and me, or even between you and two different theologies, or even between you and two different churches. It's a matter between you and Him."

When it came time for dinner, Libby was uncharacteristically quiet. She had planned to engage all the House-bugs in a religious dialogue that evening, asking them all sorts of probing questions. Instead, she excused herself, went home early, found a Catholic church that was still open, and prayed in front of the little red sanctuary light over the altar that signified His presence there. She prayed more seriously than she had ever prayed before. When she left the church, she didn't have a clear answer, and there were no miracles. But she had a sense of rightness and peace even in her uncertainty. And she knew why: because she had put her mind and heart in His hands.

Dialogue Ten

AUTHORITY

As promised, Libby met Mother one more day on the beach. The wind and the waves were both stronger than they had been any of the other days, and not many people were in the water, though a few hardy souls were body-surfing with gusto. Mother had brought a variety of bread, fruit, and tea.

Libby's first words were, "What's on our agenda for today, Mother, besides your delicious food? I don't know for sure where I stand yet, but if I do decide that what you say is all true, if I do climb every rung of the ladder so far, what next? I can't guess what the next rung is. If I become a Catholic because I'm a Christian, what do I become because I'm a Catholic?"

"A good one instead of a bad one. A whole one instead of half a one."

"But that's not another rung. That's just putting my whole foot on the Catholic rung."

"Right. But many people cut that last rung in half, and leave the half they don't like behind. You have to decide whether to do that or not."

"You mean I have to decide how completely I'm going to practice what I believe?"

"Well, yes, that too, but I was thinking of something else first. First you have to decide how completely you *believe* what you believe."

"How can someone believe something but not believe it?"

"The same way you call a woman your mama yet you not eat all the food she puts on your plate. But some people pick at Mommy's food, and eat only what they like. I call them 'cafeteria Catholics'."

"But if it's all good food because it's all from Christ— if the Church is His way of getting His food to us, and if He's God—then why would anyone want to send some of that God-food back? I don't even want to miss any of *your* delicious breads, and you're only human."

"Because they don't find it delicious."

"So it's a matter of taste."

"Yes. They judge their Mother's cooking by their taste instead of judging their own taste by their Mother."

"But if there's bad stuff in the food, how can it be from God?"

"They say it isn't. They say that the stuff they like is from God, and the stuff they don't like isn't."

"So they're judging what God says by what they say."

"They say it can't be what God says."

"Because it's not what they say."

"Yes."

"So they change it."

"Yes. That's why there's a tenth choice, a tenth rung of the ladder."

"So those who climb only up to the ninth rung— these 'cafeteria Catholics'—they believe that the Catholic Faith really is from God, right? That's the only reason they're on the ninth rung, right?"

"Right."

"So they believe the mail is from God, yet they don't want to open some of the envelopes. That doesn't make sense."

"They don't think all of it is from God. They don't think all of what the Church says is from God."

"And they figure out what part is and what part isn't by their own thinking. *They* draw the line. They don't let God draw the line."

"Yes."

"How can they teach the Faith to kids then, if they don't believe it all themselves? They'd either have to teach what they don't believe—that it's all true—and that would be a sin against their own conscience—or else they'd have to teach these Catholic kids what they *do* believe: that part of the Catholic Faith is false—and that would be a sin against justice, because the Church is trusting them to teach Catholicism, not their own personal opinions. Her authority has to judge theirs, not vice versa."

"You see the point very clearly, Libby."

"I think I picked up the habit of thinking simply from you, Mother." Libby smiled. "So, they want to edit God's mail instead of delivering it intact. What parts of it do they want to edit out?"

"Well, today it's almost always one thing: the Church's teachings about sexual morality, especially one encyclical, *Humanae Vitae*."

"That's the one where the Pope made contraception wrong, right?"

"Wrong. He didn't make it wrong. God made it wrong. The Pope didn't change anything. The Church had always said it was wrong. He just tried to explain why the Church has always taught that."

"Well, the Church *has* made some moral mistakes in the past, hasn't it? Like the Crusades and the Inquisition?"

"Mistakes in practice, certainly. But not mistakes in teaching. And even when the Church's practice was wicked, her teaching didn't change. You see, God didn't promise to keep His Church free from *sin*, but from *error*. He gave us an infallible road map but not infallible drivers. He didn't say to His Apostles, 'He who lives like you, lives like Me', but 'He who hears you, hears Me'."

"So the Church is saying, 'Do as I say, not as I do. But isn't that hypocrisy?—not practicing what you preach?"

"No, that's honest human weakness. The only two people who perfectly practice what they preach are God and cynics. God lives His ideals, and cynics have none. Not practicing what you preach isn't hypocrisy. Hypocrisy is not *believing* what you preach. That's dishonesty."

"So there's always a gap between the preaching and the practice."

"Until Heaven, yes, that's the way it is. Unfortunately, we're not in Heaven yet, even though it seems pretty nice down here today, especially if you like body-surfing."

"Even the Apostles were less than perfect role models, then."

"Are you kidding? Ever hear of Judas Iscariot? He was one of the Apostles! And the first Pope, Peter, denied Jesus, at His trial. And all the other Apostles ran away and left Him to die, except John. It's not a pretty story. Down through the centuries, wicked Catholics did wicked things: persecuted Jews, and compromised with slavery, and sacked Constantinople, and burned heretics, and embezzled money, and raped altar boys. But they knew that was wicked because the Church kept *teaching* that right was right and wrong was wrong. Even when they didn't practice what they preached, they kept preaching it. They kept the gap open between the preaching and the practice. The only way to close the gap is to stop preaching the high ideals you don't practice, or to practice the ideals you preach: to be a cynic or a saint. No, that's not quite right, because even the saints admit they're sinners. In fact, they complain about their sins much more than we do! Even they don't completely close the gap. Actually, come to think of it, the people who do close the gap are the 'cafeteria Catholics'. The saints try to do it the hard way, by practicing everything they preach, and they fail, but the 'cafeteria Catholics' do it the easy way, by preaching only what they practice—and they succeed. If they want to contracept, they stop teaching against contraception. If they want to fornicate, they stop teaching against fornication."

"But that's cheating. That's winning the game by changing the rules."

"Of course it is."

"I see the temptation, though. Especially about sexual morality. Fornication is fun, and guilt is a bummer."

"*All* sin looks like fun. If it didn't, we'd all be saints. Cocaine looks like fun at first too."

"So when the Church says, 'Don't do sin', that's like Mommy saying, 'Don't do drugs.' Okay, I gotcha. So what does the Church say about sexual morality? Let's look at the tenth rung."

"What she has always said."

"But today, people are ignoring it. So what is she saying today?"

"She's saying, 'What part of "Thou shalt not commit adultery" don't you understand?'"

"I guess those people would answer, 'I don't understand the contraception part.' "

"And that's why the Pope wrote *Humanae Vitae*."

"But suppose we still can't understand it? Are we supposed to just obey it blindly? 'Pray, pay, and obey'—is that what the Church is telling us to do?"

"No. There's more than that. But not less."

"What more?"

"Understand it. Have a good reason for obeying."

"But aren't there some Catholics who read that encyclical and still can't understand why it has to be that way, right?"

"Yes."

"So *for them*, it's just, 'Stop thinking and just obey'?"

"No. If they've climbed up the other nine rungs of the ladder, they have *reasons* to obey. (It's one reason, really, with nine steps in it.) They have *reason* for believing in the authority of the Church when she corrects their own reasoning. In fact, if their reason was enough all by itself—if after thinking about contraception with their own reason they all came to the same conclusion, the same conclusion the Church came to—then they wouldn't need the Church, would they? We need the authority of the Church when our reason *isn't* enough."

"But if it isn't reason that makes the non-cafeteria Catholics believe *Humanae Vitae*, then it's blind faith. So we're back to 'Pray, pay, and obey.' "

"No we're not. We're back to our ladder. It's a ladder of *reasons* for accepting the Church's authority. Reasons for trusting Mommy even when you don't understand her."

"It's hard for me to be satisfied with that."

"Oh, you shouldn't be! You should then try to understand it. But until you do, believe it and obey it."

"So there are two stages."

"Yes. In fact, there are three. First, you reason your way to accepting the Church's authority, as we did on our ladder. You let your reason lead to faith. Then, you accept the Faith even when it tells you things your reason hasn't understood yet. That's the faith step that the reason step led to. Last, you come to understand the Faith better, *after* you believe it. So that's the deeper reason step that faith led you to. You're not going to understand *all* of it, but you are going to understand much more than you ever could have understood in stage one, without the Church's authority to help you."

"Let me get this straight. So in stage one, reason leads to faith and in stage three, faith leads to reason."

"Yes. But that's not just some ideal scheme in the abstract, those are the three actual stages most converts actually go through. And they'll all tell you that if you ask them. That's the experience."

"So most Catholics today who accept *Humanae Vitae* are in stage two about contraception, then, right?"

"Yes, but they're gradually moving into stage three."

"And the 'cafeteria Catholics' are in stage one and *won't* move on to stage two."

"Right. But maybe some pope* will get these stage-one Catholics into stage two by writing something against

* These conversations take place in 1977, just before the election of Pope John Paul II in 1978, the year Libby and Mother meet again in *An Ocean Full of Angels*. Mother's prophetic reference points to John Paul II's encyclical *Veritatis Splendor* and to his "Theology of the Body", which is the Church's response to the sexual revolution, and the most important theological development of our time. If I may add a personal note here, I have never met a single Christian—Protestant or Catholic—who studied John Paul II's "Theology of the Body" who has not fallen in love with it. Study it, and you will be on fire to spread its joyful gospel ("good news").

relativism, and then maybe he'll also get the stage-two Catholics into stage three by writing something that gives them a deeper understanding that explains *Humanae Vitae* better."

"So the Church will change?"

"Not as you change your clothes, but as your body changes. She doesn't become another body; she just grows, from within. New clothes come from outside. And the Church grows in response to new needs. Every one of the Church's creeds is a new, deeper restatement of what she always believed, in response to some new heresy that denied it."

"So the Church is both progressive and conservative."

"If you want to use those categories, yes. But she doesn't say, 'Believe it because it's old', *or* 'Believe it because it's new', but 'Believe it because it's true.' All her creeds were her answers to heresies. The creeds about Christ said No to the heresies that denied His full divinity and then also to the heresies that denied His full humanity. The creeds about the Trinity said No to the heresies that denied God's one-ness in nature and then also to the heresies that denied the threeness of the Divine Persons. But today, the heresies aren't theological so much as they are moral. They're not mistakes about God so much as mistakes about man. They deny the dignity of man and the sanctity of human life. And the mas-ter heresy that does that, and that has taken most of our civilization along with it, is the sexual revolution."

"Why do you think that's the biggie?"

"Because we have the biggest emotional stake in it. That's the subjective reason. Objectively, it's because sex is the origin of human life itself."

"So you really think the sexual revolution is the most radical revolution that ever happened?"

"No, Christianity is that. But the sexual revolution is more radical than any merely political revolution. Because it has already overcome the strongest instinct in nature, a mother's instinct to protect her children."

"What do you mean?"

"I mean abortion. Can you imagine how amazed our ancestors would be if they found out that we made abortion legal, and millions of mothers had their babies killed every year? Almost one out of every three babies in America is killed by abortion. That's the biggest genocide in history. We murder a third of our own citizens. And why? Because of sex, because of the sexual revolution."

"How is abortion about sex?"

"Why does any woman want an abortion? Because contraception failed. Abortion is backup contraception. And why does she want contraception? Because she wants to have sex without having babies. That's what contraception *is*. If babies came without sex, if you could order them from the stork, how many abortions do you think there would be? Abortion is about contraception. Abortion is about sex."

"Why doesn't everybody see that?"

"It's like the elephant in the living room. It's too big and too embarrassing to admit. So we just look away. And maybe we're embarrassed at what our ancestors would think of us, so we don't think of them either; we ignore our history. The Church is the only voice of our ancestors that's left. Every Christian in the world believed contraception was wrong for nineteen hundred years, until the Anglicans changed the rule and allowed it, at the Lambeth Conference in 1930. And now every Christian church allows it—except the Catholic Church.

"It's the same thing with divorce", Mother continued. "There's another fruit of the sexual revolution. The Catholic Church is the only institution left that says No to divorce—because Jesus said No to divorce. In all four Gospels, yet. But because of the sexual revolution, everybody else says Yes to it, including all the Protestant churches. But the Catholic Church doesn't have that authority, the authority to contradict Jesus, to correct His teaching.

"And divorce is about sex too, of course", Mother pointed out. "Do you think it would be tolerated if it wasn't? Is there anything else that does what divorce does that would be tolerated if it didn't have anything to do with sex?"

"What do you mean, 'does what divorce does'?"

"I mean three things. It lies and cheats on the most solemn promise you make in your life to the person you say you love the most. So, one, it's betrayal. It abuses and harms your innocent children and scars them for life. So, two, it's child abuse. And it destroys your society, because no society has ever lasted without stable marriages. So, three, it's societal murder."

"Why do you think society can't last without stable marriages?"

"Isn't it obvious? If you can't be trusted to keep the most solemn, important promise in your life to the most important person in your life, how can you be trusted to keep any other promise? And how can society survive if people can't be trusted to keep their promises? All contracts, all laws, all order becomes uncertain then."

"Wow. And this all comes from the sexual revolution?"

"Well, just think about it. Imagine it was proved that something else did those three terrible things, and that something had nothing to do with sex—drinking coffee, say, or doing yoga. It would be absolutely rejected. But divorce isn't—except by the Catholic Church. You see, the sexual revolution trumps everything, even your responsibility to your spouse and your responsibility to your children and your responsibility to your society. And it's so strong that even among Catholics *Humanae Vitae* is the most hated and rejected and disobeyed encyclical in history. It's a touchstone. All 'cafeteria Catholics' reject it; all faithful Catholics accept it."

"Mother, are you saying that 'cafeteria Catholicism' is illogical? That logically faith has to be all or nothing?"

"Logically, yes. You either trust Mother or not. And if you do, then you don't pick at your food. You eat everything she puts on your plate, gratefully, even when it tastes strange. You trust her."

"Why should I trust her that much?"

"Because she is the very body of Christ, who is God."

"Then how can there be so many 'cafeteria Catholics'?"

"There is no such thing, really. It's a contradiction in terms. *Catholic* means 'universal', or 'whole', or 'all'. *Cafeteria* means only 'some'. It means being picky and choosy. You know what the Greek word for 'pick and choose' is?"

"No. What?"

"*Heretic.*"

"Oops."

"Too bad heretics don't say 'oops', like you did."

"So it's all or nothing then, the whole ladder or none of it, because ..."

"Because it's a one-piece ladder."

"But you *can* stop on any of the rungs."

"You can."

"Why not here, then? Why not stop at the last rung?"

"Because you've already bought an elephant, in climbing this high. Why balk at buying a ladybug? Especially if it's a ladybug *on that elephant*?—on the elephant that you've already bought?"

"Can you say that without all the metaphors?"

"What the Church says about sex is an integral part of what the Church says. If you've really taken Step Nine, you have to take Step Ten because Step Nine means trusting Mother, and Step Ten means trusting Mother's map for sex. And the reason you trust Mother is that she is the body and voice of Christ. And He is God. If you refuse Step Ten, you have to justify it by refusing Step Nine, and so on, back and back, and pretty soon you'll find that the only consistent position is refusing the whole ladder, refusing Step One. And that's where so many people are. Which is nowhere."

"If the tenth step is so small, why do most Catholics in America refuse it? It obviously doesn't look like a ladybug to them."

"It would if they had really taken all the other steps. They see it as a big obstacle only because they're an inch away from it. Your thumb can look bigger than the sun if you put it right in front of your eye. Back up, get a sense of perspective, and you'll see it differently."

"That may be logical, but it's not easy. It takes time, that sense of perspective."

"Yes it does. Did you think I was expecting an instant conversion, like a Fundamentalist altar call?"

"Thanks for understanding that. You know, when I ask myself honestly, 'Am I totally convinced of each step of the ladder or not?' I have to answer both Yes and No."

"That's not surprising. That's what the man in the Gospels said: 'Lord, I believe; help Thou my unbelief.' "

"So doubts aren't just killed and turned into corpses and buried, then? They're like bugs that keep bugging you?"

"They're like the ants in the pants of faith that keep it alive and moving. It's not alive unless it's moving. Intellectual doubts are like moral temptations: they're our sparring partners that keep our muscles in shape."

"Does it always have to be a struggle? Is it never a peace, a certainty?"

"It can be both. Like a marriage."

"It's really complicated—the psychology of it, I mean."

"Yes. Because the soul is divided into three powers—mind, will, and emotions—and they're often divided among themselves. The soul is like a ship, and the will is like the captain, and the captain often listens to the sailors—the desires, the passions, the emotions, the imagination—more than to the navigator, the mind."

"So the Church is all three things for us?"

"No. She can't be our will any more than she can be our emotions. She can only inform our mind. Because God has put the steering wheel of the ship into our own hands in giving us that fearful and wonderful gift of free will. 'The Church only proposes, not imposes.' "

"Like a marriage proposal."

"Yes."

"And it's also a ladder."

"Yes."

"That's a really mixed metaphor."

"Not if the ladder is Romeo's ladder to get Juliet to come and elope with him."

"I like the metaphor of the marriage proposal better. The ladder is only a thing, not a person."

"No. It's a person."

"What? Who?"

"To discover its secret identity—the identity of every step of the way you have taken during these past ten days—read Genesis 28:12 and then John 1:51."

"I'll look it up."

"And the rest of the Book is pretty good too. And full of surprises."

AFTERWORD

This fictional dialogue (like the novel from which its characters were taken) takes place in the 1970s. Mother's last prophecy came true in 1978 when John Paul the Great became Pope. Among his astonishing achievements was saving the world from nuclear war, winning the Cold War for the West, and ending the reign of communism in the U.S.S.R. Others played essential roles in that drama too, of course, notably Reagan, Gorbachev, and Margaret Thatcher, but John Paul II was the major player, even on a natural, human level, forgetting about the just-as-real and far-more-powerful supernatural causes.

But even this achievement was a small thing compared to an intellectual achievement that may have been the Church's greatest theological contribution since Saint Thomas Aquinas: John Paul's answer—that is, Mother Church's answer—to the sexual revolution, namely, the "Theology of the Body". Almost everyone who has seriously studied it has come away impressed, convinced, moved, and changed, in both thought and life. This book is a preliminary for that, a "salesman's pitch".

As Saint George's importance is relative to the dragon's, and Dr. Von Helsing's importance is relative to Dracula's, so the importance of the "Theology of the Body" is relative to the importance of the sexual revolution.

The importance of that revolution, in turn, is relative to the importance of the blood which this Dracula is draining away, namely, the lifeblood of marriage and the family.

The importance of this institution, in turn, is relative to the importance of the thing of which it is the absolutely first and indispensable foundation, namely, all of human society—in fact, all of human life on earth.

I think God cares even more about the family than about the Church, for families without a Church are like a fertile field without seeds, but a Church without families is like seeds without a field.

Why is Islam conquering Europe? Because they are having families and Christians are not. Why is Western civilization dying? Why are Islam and Mormonism, both serious heresies, growing faster than Christianity everywhere in Western civilization? I think it is because God cares even more about orthopraxy than about orthodoxy, even more about families than about theology, and because He keeps His promise, made by all the prophets, to bless those who obey His laws and punish those who do not. Muslims and Mormons are keeping most of God's commandments better than Christians are in today's world, especially the ones about sex, marriage, and family, the ones that are the cause of all the "dissent" in the Church today.

Of course, there is the problem about the Muslim track record concerning that one bothersome little Commandment that says something like *Thou shalt not murder*. And if you don't have that, if you don't have life, you can't have anything else. The right to life is the first of rights. But apart from that, the score is *Muslims*: 9, *Christians*: 1. And even regarding murder, we kill more innocent people in American abortion clinics in one day than all the hateful and hate-filled Muslim terrorists in the world kill in a year.

APPENDIX

The medievals reveled in order, in structure, in connections, in analogies. Many people still do. They often find mathematics fascinating, even if they are not good at it, because of its wonderful order. For those who like this kind of thing, I have provided a chart of all the possible permutations and combinations among the ten steps in my argument, or rungs on my ladder. It shows all the possible alternatives to simply moving straight ahead "onward and upward" through all ten steps. (Notice that there are two kinds of alternatives: climbing too few rungs and climbing too many rungs too early.)

Readers who enjoy doing this sort of thing can fill in the details of the psychological profile of the persons who find themselves in each of the alternatives, and they can find examples of such persons both in literature and in life. There are people who fit into each of these boxes.

If you hate "little boxes" (i.e., order and classification, especially of people), please do not fulminate but just ignore this as a harmless game whose fascination you simply cannot understand. Like most Americans, I simply cannot understand how the English can possibly be fascinated with cricket, so I just leave this mystery to God and the English. The English usually feel the same way about American baseball.

There are ninety possible boxes with a "without" in their label, and each of these is an alternative to climbing all ten steps of the ladder. Exactly forty-five of the boxes (the "southwest" corner of the diagram) are partial, or incomplete: lower steps of the ladder without the higher steps; while the other forty-five (the "northeast" corner) are hasty, or cheating: higher steps without the lower, foundational ones.

	PASSION	TRUTH	MEANING	LOVE	LAW
PASSION		TRUTH WITHOUT PASSION	MEANING WITHOUT PASSION	LOVE WITHOUT PASSION	LAW WITHOUT PASSION
TRUTH	PASSION WITHOUT TRUTH		MEANING WITHOUT TRUTH	LOVE WITHOUT TRUTH	LAW WITHOUT TRUTH
MEANING	PASSION WITHOUT MEANING	TRUTH WITHOUT MEANING		LOVE WITHOUT MEANING	LAW WITHOUT MEANING
LOVE	PASSION WITHOUT LOVE	TRUTH WITHOUT LOVE	MEANING WITHOUT LOVE		LAW WITHOUT LOVE
LAW	PASSION WITHOUT LAW	TRUTH WITHOUT LAW	MEANING WITHOUT LAW	LOVE WITHOUT LAW	
GOD	PASSION WITHOUT GOD	TRUTH WITHOUT GOD	MEANING WITHOUT GOD	LOVE WITHOUT GOD	LAW WITHOUT GOD
JEWS	PASSION WITHOUT JEWS	TRUTH WITHOUT JEWS	MEANING WITHOUT JEWS	LOVE WITHOUT JEWS	LAW WITHOUT JEWS
CHRIST	PASSION WITHOUT CHRIST	TRUTH WITHOUT CHRIST	MEANING WITHOUT CHRIST	LOVE WITHOUT CHRIST	LAW WITHOUT CHRIST
CHURCH	PASSION WITHOUT CHURCH	TRUTH WITHOUT CHURCH	MEANING WITHOUT CHURCH	LOVE WITHOUT CHURCH	LAW WITHOUT CHURCH
AUTHORITY	PASSION WITHOUT AUTHORITY	TRUTH WITHOUT AUTHORITY	MEANING WITHOUT AUTHORITY	LOVE WITHOUT AUTHORITY	LAW WITHOUT AUTHORITY

GOD	JEWS	CHRIST	CHURCH	AUTHORITY
GOD WITHOUT PASSION	JEWS WITHOUT PASSION	CHRIST WITHOUT PASSION	CHURCH WITHOUT PASSION	AUTHORITY WITHOUT PASSION
GOD WITHOUT TRUTH	JEWS WITHOUT TRUTH	CHRIST WITHOUT TRUTH	CHURCH WITHOUT TRUTH	AUTHORITY WITHOUT TRUTH
GOD WITHOUT MEANING	JEWS WITHOUT MEANING	CHRIST WITHOUT MEANING	CHURCH WITHOUT MEANING	AUTHORITY WITHOUT MEANING
GOD WITHOUT LOVE	JEWS WITHOUT LOVE	CHRIST WITHOUT LOVE	CHURCH WITHOUT LOVE	AUTHORITY WITHOUT LOVE
GOD WITHOUT LAW	JEWS WITHOUT LAW	CHRIST WITHOUT LAW	CHURCH WITHOUT LAW	AUTHORITY WITHOUT LAW
	JEWS WITHOUT GOD	CHRIST WITHOUT GOD	CHURCH WITHOUT GOD	AUTHORITY WITHOUT GOD
GOD WITHOUT JEWS		CHRIST WITHOUT JEWS	CHURCH WITHOUT JEWS	AUTHORITY WITHOUT JEWS
GOD WITHOUT CHRIST	JEWS WITHOUT CHRIST		CHURCH WITHOUT CHRIST	AUTHORITY WITHOUT CHRIST
GOD WITHOUT CHURCH	JEWS WITHOUT CHURCH	CHRIST WITHOUT CHURCH		AUTHORITY WITHOUT CHURCH
GOD WITHOUT AUTHORITY	JEWS WITHOUT AUTHORITY	CHRIST WITHOUT AUTHORITY	CHURCH WITHOUT AUTHORITY